Lessons Every Goddess Must Know

LEONIE DAWSON

t

ISBN: 1496067967
ISBN-13: 978-1496067968

DEDICATION

For every woman who has ever felt lost, alone & without her angels.
For every woman who wondered where her light had gone.
For every woman who knew there must be a better way.
For every woman who remembered a Goddess lived inside her

ACKNOWLEDGMENTS

Gratitude to my amazing team.
Colossal love & gratitude to all my Amazing Biz and Life Academy sisters.

My hunky love Christian who believes in me without a doubt.
My daughter Ostara who shines brighter than a star
and our new little baby mermaid.

And most of all, to Great Spirit & this beautiful world
for being pretty much the best thing ever.

Dearest Goddess,

Welcome.

Welcome to this sacred playbook, to this adventure, to this rainbow tiedyed quilt of all the things that make my heart sing.

But most of all, welcome to this way of life.

When I was 21, I stepped foot into a women's circle.

I met my spiritual mentors and my soul sisters.

And in one moment, I knew I had come.

I knew I was a goddess.

My life made sense – more than it had ever made.

Since that time all those years ago, I've dedicated my life to remembering just what a radiant, sacred, joyful, creative goddess I am.

And I'm standing here before you, clad in turquoise & sea shells , here to help you remember too.

The moment you know you are a Goddess, your life begins to change. Life becomes magical. Deeper. Richer. More glorious than you could ever imagine. You'll laugh deeper. You'll be spellbound by beauty. You'll make powerful, strong choices that will nourish you. You'll feel inspired, enraptured. You'll be giddy in love with yourself. You'll create miracles.

In short – you'll feel aglow.

And everyone around you? They'll see it and feel it too.

May this book play a part on your journey of seeing, remembering & being the Goddess in You.

From every cell in my being, I want you to know:

You are a Goddess.

Sacred. Divine. Beautiful. Whole.

I am here for you.

I believe in you.

All my love,

Leonie

How to Use This Book.

Write in it. Mark it. Love it.

Sleep with it. Soak in it. Nibble. Chew. Gulp.

Colour it in. Write your story in it. Make notes.

Make tea. Make love. Make it your own.

Read it from cover to cover.

Dive in dive out.

Only nibble as your heart desires.

Let a page open for you like an oracle.

Let it soothe you, guide you, show you a new way.

Let it be a playbook, a sacred sanctuary,

a date with

the Goddess in You.

How to be a goddess

Trust your intuition ☆ Dream big ☆ Do big ♡ believe in your gifts ☽ Have faith ◎ See yourself as radiant ☆ Check in with your wisdom ♡ Speak of the good in this world & in others ☆ Let the sun kiss you ◡ Speak to your angels ◎ Make joy ☼ Play with the child inside you ✿ Know yourself as beautiful ☆ Trust that everything will turn out wonderfully ☽ Be your highest self.

Inside you there is the

wise one

the shamaness

the dreamer

the lover

the creator

the wife

the mother

the daughter

the sister

the artist

the one who knows best

the one who knows all manner of things in this world

can be healed with a cup of tea, with an hour of listening,

with those lightbeams we call love

and sisterhood.

Inside you there is

A Goddess.

Beautiful. Wise. True. Divine.

(Can you feel her?)

JOYFUL GODDESS

50 Ways

to Feel Like a Goddess Again

Let's make a list. And come back to it every time we need to remember, mkay? It doesn't take long to remember just what luscious, shining goddesses we are.

Take a meditation-nap

Have a green smoothie! Greens are good for the soul AND our moods!

Reach out to five people and tell them how much you love them and are grateful for them.

Go for a drive to a place you haven't been before... Even if it's just a road, park, shop or river. Let your spirit see new things!

Switch off your computer for the day and remember joys which are screen-free.

Write your Things to do this Life list.

Create something just for you...

Write a love letter to the Goddess in You.

Give away or donate three things you own that don't make you feel magical.

Watch inspiring movies

... or watch ridiculous 1980s comedies or silly romantic-comedies or kid's movies... feel good movies!

Me at 14... sunset on the farm

Stand outside when it is sunset or sunrise... the colours and light will heal your chakras and energy...

Create a dreamboard.

Dream up, organise and host a gathering of goddesses.

Make a raw dessert.

Find a place you can have a campfire. You don't have to camp out all night... just stay for the best bits of fire-gazing and marshmallow-burning!

Mark in your calendar an LBW. My hunky invented these – Lazy Bastard Weekends. A weekend where you have total permission to do as little as possible. In pyjamas. Then nap. It's muchos healing and restorative!

Ask your Mama to tell you your birth story.

Whenever I am in need of healing, I read SARK's "Transformation Soup". It's my favourite of hers to bring joy, healing & rejuvenation into my life. Sparkle SARKle!

Get a reading by someone you either know already, or who comes recommended. Readings always help me get back on track again when I lose my way.

Go swimming. Even if swimming just means sitting in the spa at your local health club. That totally counts!

Drink more water. Chances are you are dehydrated. Love your friendly water police!

Stop complaining for today. Start saying you are AWESOME... You will begin to feel it!

Give your crystals a good cleansing with water and salt, sunlight or moonlight.

Decide to forgive someone.

See if you can find music you were obsessed by as a kid or teen. (My sisters know all the words to the Lion King soundtrack! I was more in love with Rick Price, Ace of Bass and Joshua Kadison). Listen to them again... maybe even sing along!

Make a pile of your favourite healing books and lie in amongst them.

Find a crystal and make it your healing crystal. Keep it in your pocket during the day, sleep beside it at night. Let it become a beloved companion! Amethyst, jade and green calcite are especially good healers, but trust your intuition as to what YOU need!

Thank someone from your past who was special to you. (I once wrote a letter to my fourth grade teacher Miss Collins thanking her for making a gifted and talented writers class and asking me along. That class meant so much to me!)

Make space in your life for magic to enter by doing some divine decluttering!

Go on a retreat. One that's run by you, or a group one. Retreats are oh so good!

Organise a breakfast date with your favourite person.

Decide on a new hobby to play with that you haven't tried before... Horse riding! Scrap booking! Disco bowling! Knitting! Ice skating! Creative writing! Ze possibilities are endless...

Cuddle a puppy or meow-meow.

Marry yourself.

Create an altar that feels supportive, uplifting and inspiring... a collection of all the lovely things you want to remind yourself of...

Create a gift basket for your best friend.

Take 100 deep breaths. One after the other.

Find your totem animal.

Go have a book picnic outside and get distracted by the clouds!

Make your bedroom into a sanctuary.

Give yourself a superhero name for ze day! I am Queen Megatron! I can bounce with the power of a thousand pogo sticks and a hundred Tiggers!

Take yourself on an Artist's Date for lunch!

Let someone else decide what book you should read next.

Paint an angel and put it beside your bed.

- Sleep in the moonlight – either keep your curtains open or sleep outside. Or if you can't do either – step outside for a moment before going to bed just to say goodnight to Grandmother Moon.

- Take a media break.

- Write on a piece of paper what you are willing to let go of. Burn it.

- Write letters. The kind that need stamps. Apply stickers by ze boatload. Embrace your inner penpalling eleven year old self!

- Play dress-ups.

- Make one new friend for the day – who cares if it is online or offline. Connection is goooood!

Write a list of your own favourite ways to heal and get sparkly again...

You are beautiful
just as you are.
Inside you is a
spunky star-filled
soul that shines
through your skin,
lighting you up
like a chinese
lantern.
You are a firefly
lighting the night
sky, you're a prayer,
a gift, a dream come true...

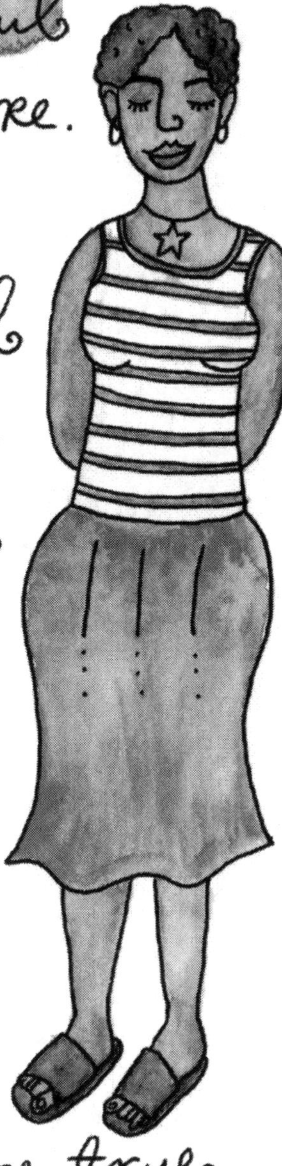

You have permission

Today, and everyday, you have permission.

You have permission

Today, and everyday, you have permission.

You have permission to say no to demands on your time that don't light you up, and don't give energy back to you.

You have permission to not give a crap what's happening outside your world, and keep your energy focussed on what you are creating.

You have permission to let go of friendships that make you feel like shit.

You have permission to say no whenever you like, however you like, in whatever kind of voice you like, without feeling like only Mean Girls Say No and Nice Girls Say Yes. That's bull. Yes and No have equal weighting – what's important is if you use them when they are the best thing for you, not out of fear, obligation or guilt.

You have permission to know that Yes is powerful, and so is No. The power comes from you using either from your highest spirit and truest integrity.

You have permission to change. You have permission to not be the person you once were.

You have permission to get angry and self-righteous, and to also glean the wisdom from those emotions. They are leading you to where your boundaries are, and where they have been crossed, and what you need to do from now on.

You have permission to be exactly how you are.

You have permission to not be more like anyone else in the world, even if you think they are better, wiser or more popular. You have permission to be more like yourself, your gifts and your wisdom.

You have permission to not care what other people think of you.

You have permission to not try to change what other people think of you. You can't ever argue that you are a good person. They will either know you are, or not. You don't need to spend time with people who don't believe in you.

You have permission to do things that your friends and family do not.

You have permission to be wild, expressive, truthful, exciting and outspoken.

You have permission to not accept friendship requests on Facebook, or anywhere else in your life. You have permission to block people whenever you like.

You have permission to share as much or as little as you like. You have permission to blog, or not blog. You have permission to Twitter, or not to Twitter. It doesn't really matter. As long as it's making you happy, that's the best thing.

You have permission to suck at a wide variety of activities. It's okay. You make up for it with your million other brilliance particles.

You have permission to be whatever body shape you like.

You have permission to choose, and choose again. And then choose again.

You have permission to not always be a perfect image of something.

You have permission to be a contradiction.

You have permission to not go to your school reunion, unless it really excites you and delights you, and you would love to really heart-reconnect with people you went to school with.

You have permission to not be interested in the newest fad: harem pants, geek glasses, polaroid cameras, scrapbooking, macrame. You also have permission to be totally obsessed with them, if it makes your heart light up.

You have permission to cut people from your life. You have permission to surround yourself with people who are good and loving and nurturing to you.

You have permission to be a disappointment to some people, as long as you're not a disappointment to yourself.

You have permission to do nothing whenever you like.

You have permission to make your big dream come true.

You have permission to not do it all perfectly, or have all your shit together.

You have permission to not forgive people. You have permission to forgive people when it's right for you.

You have permission to think some people are crazy. You have permission to think some people are smigging ice-cream with chocolate and wafers and sprinkles and cherries on top.

You have permission to not have the perfect relationship.

You have permission to not have a relationship.

You have permission to take whatever time you need for you.

You have permission to make ridiculous choices for yourself.

You have permission to use and listen to your intuition. To feel when things are off, and to remove yourself from them, even when you don't quite know why. You will always find out why. Our intuition is here to serve us.

You have permission to be down. You have permission to be up.

You have permission to still believe in unicorns and fairies.

You have permission to believe in things that other people think are very very odd and strange. You have permission to not care. You have permission to believe in things that make your life wholer, richer and deeper. You have permission to make your own world that is the truest painting of you.

You have permission to suck at colouring in.

You have permission to say bugger off to anyone who has ever told you that you're not good enough, you're not worth it, you are not beautiful, you are not lovable and you are not the most divine, wise, delicious Goddess to walk the planet.

You have permission to know that you are.

You have permission to swear when you like, however you like, to your reckless abandon.

You have permission to not be the best of anything – just the best of yourself. And some days, just the best you can do that day.

You have permission to not always give. You have permission to fill your own cup up first.

You have permission to have things around you that delight you.

You have permission to live in a tipi if you want to, or a mansion. Whatever makes your spirit shine is the right thing for you.

You have permission to make choices on whether it makes your spirit shine.

You have permission to know you are a goddess, even when it doesn't feel like it. Even when you feel utterly human. Even when you want nothing more than to climb under your blanket, or light up the sky.

You are a goddess.

You have permission.

You have permission.

You have permission.

What do you need to give yourself permission for?

If you were a SUPERHERO, what would you be a SUPERHERO of?

Circle every word that describes you.

Fabulous
glorious
Kooky
MAGNIFICENT
Artsy
Fantastic
INCREDIBLE
Delicious
Creative
Dreamy
An Angel
Divine
Heart Soaked
EXQUISITE
Adored
Pure magic.
Super Special
Adorable
a goddess!
A Fairy
a dream come true
Capable of a miracle
Wise
Safe
Blessed.
A Lightworker
A Soul's yes

(Hint: You are all these things & more, dearest ♥)

how did you get blessed?

Dear You,

Hello beautiful soul.

I'm writing this to you... any soul who has been going through a dark night of the soul.

I know it's been a big time.

Heart-breaking. Transformation. Loss. Letting Go. Being tested again and again.

Some of the strongest relationships I know have been pulled at, over and over.

I know some souls have chosen to leave the planet. Some have gone willingly. For some, it was just the time for the rainbow journey.

So much loss. So much sadness. So much letting go.

I know you might have lost everything, then lost a little more.

I know you might have found the bottom of the faith barrel, and are scraping for remnants.

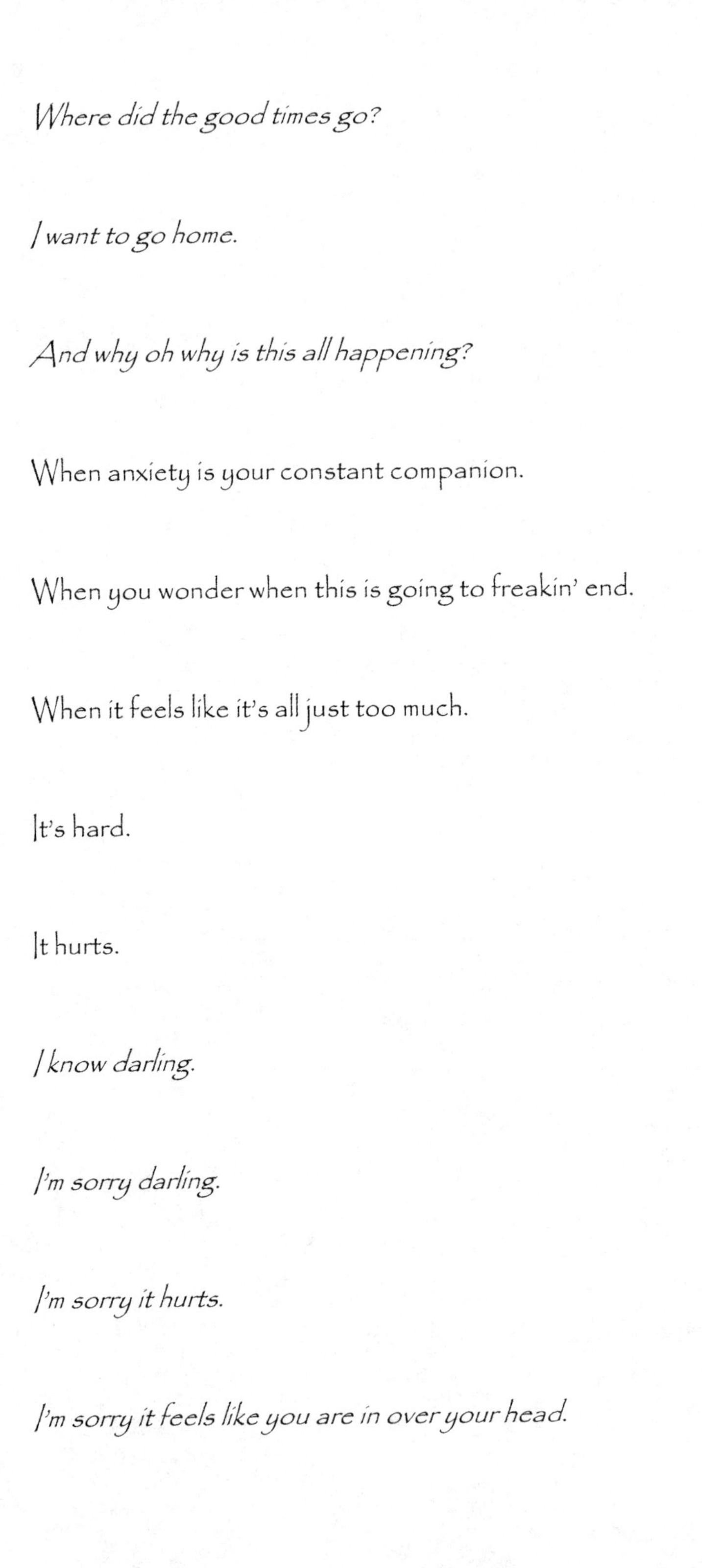

Where did the good times go?

I want to go home.

And why oh why is this all happening?

When anxiety is your constant companion.

When you wonder when this is going to freakin' end.

When it feels like it's all just too much.

It's hard.

It hurts.

I know darling.

I'm sorry darling.

I'm sorry it hurts.

I'm sorry it feels like you are in over your head.

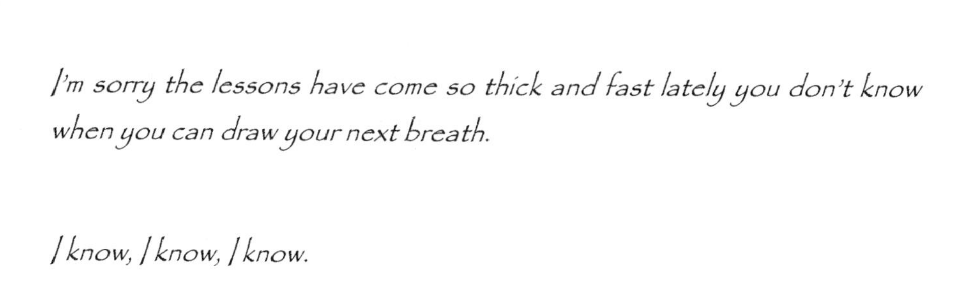

I'm sorry the lessons have come so thick and fast lately you don't know when you can draw your next breath.

I know, I know, I know.

I'm sorry.

I love you.

I want to knock on the door of every soul's house that is hurting. I want to wrap you up in a soft, freshly washed blanket. I want to give you nourishing, healing tea... blends that are made just for you and what you need.

I want to listen.

I want to whisper things to you.

I want to tell you that no matter how hard things are right now, no matter the pain, no matter the sadness... I want you to know that it's all for a reason. A good one.

And that is so hard to hear right now...

And yet... there is a mountain of faith inside me. One that glows and glides and sings.

At night, as I fall into slumberland, I think of you, and send out flocks of love, riding on wings. I hope they find you where you are.

I want to remind you that you are beautiful.

That you are loved. That you have been loved from the moment two cells met and became one. That moment, that instant, that your heart became. The moment you were born. The moment that finds you right here, right now, right where you are. And all the moments in between. You have been loved. You are loved. *You will always and forever be loved.*

I want you to know that good things are on their way. That you are on the right path. That all your rough edges are being sloughed away, transforming you into the smooth, shining river stone of light that you are.

It is true.

You may not have any faith left right now, and that's okay.

I can believe for you right now. I can hold the faith for you right now.

I want you to know... oh, so many things.

I close my eyes, and try to put into words all the things I know are true...

but there are no words, there is just this *wash of love.*

This wash of love that is just for you. From me to you. From a million souls to you. Just for you.

I love you, I love you, I love you.

I'm sorry things are so hard right now.

Things will work out, darlingheart.

One day, you will look back on all of this. We will be sitting, drinking tea, and you will burst out into laughter and say:

I know what it was all for now. It got me from there to here, the place I needed to be. It got me to be the person I needed to be.

And you will be filled with Grace. With Love. With Joy. With Faith again. And every speck in the universe will light up again, because you will have seen it and known it for what it truly is...

All here for you. All here for your awakening. All here for you to come home to you, the amazing, shining, knowing soul you are.

I believe in you. Over and over.

I love you. A thousand million times.

You are not alone, dearest.

This is all for good.

I love you so, so, so much.

Goddess Leonie

Want to feel love ♡

from your angels?

Press HERE

This healing sanctuary spot is filled with incredible magic... Your angels are waiting for you... they are HERE!

Cut, copy, colour & add to!

I believe in you...

(it's true)

You are remarkable just as you are.

YOU ARE LOVED IN A THOUSAND DIFFERENT DIRECTIONS

The Worst Thing in the World Could be the Best

When I was a child, I used to pray every night. Feverish prays, hoping that if I could name all the worst things in the world, they wouldn't happen to.

Dear God, please don't let anyone in my family die. Please stop the drought. Please don't let my parents divorce. Please don't let the cattle rustlers steal any more cattle.

Can you tell I grew up on a farm?

I kept thinking if I could stop all those very bad things from happening, then I would be happy. Then everything would be okay.

Guess what?

My brother died. The drought did keep going. And the cattle rustlers keep stealing. And years later, my parents did separate.

And still, everything was okay. And still, I found happiness.

That thing – the thing you fear the most – or that you feel is the worst thing right now?

It could end up being the very best thing.

It could end up being a ginormous blessing.

It could be a gift.

Right here – in this moment – we don't have the whole view. We can only guess that this Thing – that Very Terrible Thing – is the worst thing for us. We don't have all the information, the knowledge and the goodness of being able to look back on it... to see it was right for us, and the best thing.

When my brother died, I thought I would never be happy again. I was wrong. I did find happiness again – a happiness that was more beautiful, richer, deeper and profound than I had known before.

When I broke up with boyfriends, and my heart felt like it was broken on the kerb and I was suffocating with sadness – I could not possibly know then that it was taking me closer to finding my true love.

When my parents were devastated to have to sell my grandmother's cottage, they didn't know that it gave us the dream to buy it instead, and the gift of moving back to our homelands when our baby was born.

When a boy didn't love me back – I was given the gift of space, and the gift of promise that one day, the right boy would. And he does.

When I didn't win that prize – my life turned out superbly anyway.

When something broke, or was lost, it gave me the gift of the future, and where I needed to be.

When something I wanted desperately to happen didn't? I realise now I didn't actually need it the way I thought I did.

I see now that for all the times I fought against the universe, and raged that it hadn't given me what I wanted – that it was giving me what I truly needed all along.

It has given me medicine, healing, patience, compassion, rich spirit gifts... and it has given me myself as the woman I was born to be, and the life I was meant to lead.

This is a song for you... wherever you are... broken-hearted, lost, or embroiled in That Big Terrible Thing.

I want you to know that everything will be okay – in fact it will be utterly beautiful. And that it's okay if you don't believe me. I have enough faith to build a boat for all of us to float in.

What could feel like the Worst Thing In The World right now... could be the biggest miracle you've ever known.

I believe in you.

She let her worries drift away in the breeze, knowing that by releasing them, she was making room for blessings and miracles to enter her life...

The Secret of the Elders

Every tribe has its elders.

You know the ones. They are the ones who have navigated through long, long years of this living business.

I know older ones of course – many of them. Those who have lived, but still haven't learned.

The elders are different though. They are the ones who have not been skewed, jaded or ruptured by the thousand moments where the heart stands still, when hope is lost, when days are sodden with grief, when things do not go according to the plan.

I am blessed. I have three. Three women, all in their nineties.

My grandmother Marion. My grandmother is the youngest. She is 93. She still lives by herself, up until last year in the old wooden cottage we now live in and now in a set of sweet flats where elders circle to create ornate gardens and peer their head into each other's doors. As is the way in this small town, most of them are cousins.

My grandmother has outlived her two lovers, her two sons, and one grandson. She still works two days a week in the "boutique" – an op shop. And she dresses better than I do. She wears pearls and high heels and tight fitting, dipping bright blue dresses. She has a collection of eight retro white-rimmed sunglasses. She is uncannily intuitive – knowing before anyone else in the family (including the subject) who is falling in love, who is falling out and who needs to be told they are beautiful today.

The second (on the left) is my grandmother's sister Lucy. Lucy has deep red hair and the innocence of a fairy. She fell in love with her soulmate when she was still a teenager. He was fifteen years older, and although I don't remember him, his kindness is spoken about in glowing whispers. My mother likes to tell a story about someone complimenting Fred on his pink shirt. In return, he took it off and gave it to them. I tell this about Fred, because it tells you about Lucy too. Fred was the gentle man who made his life's work to take care of and love the red-haired, kind-hearted fairy girl who chose him. Lucy has Alzheimer's disease, and though she now doesn't remember anyone's name, it matters not – she loves them just the same. She knows you are good. She knows you are family – everyone is.

And the little old lady who lived down the road when I grew up. I know her – as does most of our small town – simply as Nan. Nan is 96, the eldest of the elders. Nan's eyes are the loveliest of blue, and she likes to ask intensive questions about computers and the internet so she can understand this funny online goddess job thing I have. I remember when I was 6, Nan and Pop left on a holiday. She returned without him by her side, a heart attack having taken her love. I remember the neighbourhood's children being gathered up to meet her on the bus, each of us holding a rose for her. She got off the bus, and cried, and held us all, then introduced us to the Swiss girl she'd made dear friends with on the bus who she'd invited to live with her for a while. And she did.

That is how my Nan is – a woman with an open heart who looks to love wherever she can.

Three women.

All in their nineties.

They have lost their parents, siblings, loves, children, grandchildren. They have lived stories untold – of miscarriages, abortions, poverty, pain, infidelity. My grandmother told me she once spent the night in prison with her family – because it was Christmas Eve, they were visiting the city, there were no hotel rooms available and they had no money. So the police took them in and let them stay the night with two young children. There have been breakdowns, suicides, alcoholism, watching children waste away for years from cancer. They have lived in tents. They have been beaten. They have lived through the bombing of London. There have been two world wars. There has been the deepest of depressions.

And yet – and yet.

These women – they glow.

They are happy.

They have a deep and ferocious faith that people are good.

They believe anything can be solved with the salve of love.

The years have not torn them asunder.

They have widened them and smoothed them like a river smooths a rock.

They glisten. They are wells of compassion, of wisdom and of laughter.

They have a secret.

I know other stories, other older ones. Those whose tapestries have warped from the threads of living, have torn and frayed and tangled. Those who haven't become beacons in their tribes. Those who have hurt more than healed. The years don't always mend and soften and deepen a person.

I wonder what separates the elders from the older.

And then I listen, and I see.

We drive with the elders.

Without fail, on the drive to the farm, my Aunt Lucy the fairy coos:

Oh! Those mountains! Look at those mountains! I've never seen anything like them! The beauty!

My grandmother is more pragmatic:

Look at this road. It's so wide and so smooth! Such a good road to travel on!

She turns to me and says:

Leonie, you are a good mum. You look beautiful today. Ostara is the most beautiful baby, isn't she the most lovely thing you've ever seen?

And your Dad, he's an old bushy, but he's got a good heart, and gosh he loves you children.

And my Nan, ever the heart, says about each and every day we have together:

Well, that was just the most wonderful day possible. I can't imagine a better day.

And on, and on, and on, these women speak, singing the praises of every little thing, every little person.

Everywhere, there are blessings, there are miracles, there is a universe tending to our million needs for air, comfort, love, support, good roads, kind hearts, tender gatherings and delicious mountains.

And they are the sentinels watching for them, praising them, delighting in them, alerting us all to them.

This is their secret.

As life's cyclones and storms and tornados tear trees and branches from limb, as earthquakes shatter and quake, as tsunamis wash and swallow, these women, they turn their faces to their sun and say:

This life is good. Just look at that beautiful sun!

May I listen, may I learn, may I know.

What sacred lessons do your elders teach you?

How to be joyful...
Decide to CHOOSE it
Make Magic wherever you go
When people ask how you Are, say "FABULOUS" & give a big grin!
Practise being Happy
Know that JOY is an artform you choose to play with, not something that happens to you.

CREATIVE GODDESS

Creative Permission

You have permission.

You have permission to create.

You have permission to follow your spirit.

You have permission to take up some messy paints and pastels, and make something new and miraculous and alive.

You have permission to be crazy-wild brave.

You have permission to not colour-between-the-lines anymore.

You have permission to fall in love with yourself.

You have permission to drop all the should-nots, and step into the things that make you light up.

You have permission to be a Goddess.

You have permission to dip your fingers, your hands, your feet in rainbow swathes of paint whenever you like.

You have permission to not be neat.

You have permission to make the art, the writings, that tell of your story, and your spirit, and your precious journey.

You have permission to make it your own.

You have permission to believe in the possibility that you are a radiant Goddess.

You have permission to make art that isn't for anyone else but you.

You have permission to really, really GET just how amazing and wise you are.

You have permission to experience joy.

You have permission to be enraptured with your own art.

You have permission to be the Creative Goddess you are.

You have permission.

You Have Permission.

Write your own Creative Permission slip here:

Art can be:

- a playground to feel FREE in
- a path of self discovery
- a sacred circle to experience the Divine
- a place of meditation
- a great healer
- the story of your soul
- a scrapbook of your miracles
- a collage of your dreams
- a necklace of prayer
- a mandala of inner peace.

Art can show us the way & the journey... how to live, who we are & what we can be.

Art can show us the goddess inside us..

The Wild Donkey Secret to Getting Stuff Done

So one of the most popular questions I get asked is...

How the heck do you manage to put so much stuff out?!

As one friend remarked to me:

You seem to be in an endless summer of creating!

She has a point.

Over the last three years, I've created:

- 4 meditation kits
- 5 e-courses
- 3 books
- 75 something videos
- 100+ original artworks
- 1500+ blog posts.

Not to mention grown my business from a hobby to a thriving enterprise that sustains my whole family. Crazy productive.

AND I also had an office job for two of those years.

Oh. AND had a baby.

So yup, I've got a gift at getting stuff done.

Want to know my secret?

It's really, really complex.

(Tee hee! It's not! It's as simple as a donkey, as all things should be!)

It's the

RIDE ZE WILD DONKEY technique.

Best.name.ever.

So, a wild donkey of an idea shows up in your paddock.

It's your job to jump on, and ride it until it's finished, done, complete-o.

And then your job is to release it into the wilds.

The donkey will have done what has needed to.

And so will have you.

Want to know how I've ridden my donkeys?

The very first Creating your Goddess Year workbook?

I came up with the idea just before Christmas of 2010. Four days of creating alldayeveryday later, it was finished and sent out into the world.

The Radiant Goddess e-course videos? Filmed over one 12 hour day.

The Creative Goddess e-course? Created SIX WEEKS of course materials (six 30 minute videos, six 30 minute original meditation MP3s and six hand-illustrated & painted workbooks) over SIX DAYS.

Bonkerdoodles?

Yes.

Crazy effective?

Yes.

Because those wild donkeys got ridden. And then they got released.

The Problem With The Chip-Away Technique

The thing is – and I suspect 97% of the population are secretly like me -

I'm not one to chip away at stuff for a year or three.

Bleh. The whole idea feels muted and dull to me.

The only guarantee out of that technique for me is that I *will* lose interest and momentum.

And yet – if I just **harness the energy of the wild donkey idea when it's in my paddock, it makes creating so much easier.**

I am happy to have days of huge creative surges then rest and recover for a week after.

What happens when I wait...

Want to know what happens to the stuff that I wait for, molly coddle, caress gently, tease out, think about, want to make perfect?

That's the stuff I haven't made.

That's the stuff that's still sitting on my desk.

It's called **Mount Project**, and it is a mammoth pile that still teases me.

Riding the wild donkey might be wild, but my gosh is it fun and exhilarating and delicious.

And oh my goddess, how it gets things DONE. Created. Out in the world for them to dance their magic and do what they need to do.

Which is much more than can be said for all the dreams that lay buried in Mount Project.

The way I see it?

It's my responsibility to ride the donkeys that turn up in my paddock.

There's something I need to learn from them.

There's something that needs to happen there.

And those wild, gorgeous crumby donkeys need me to set them free into the world.

Which I can only do by **putting on some big girl panties, a cowgirl hat & some canoes, and just** JUMPING ON.

Riding, creating, having faith, trusting, pushing, taking deep breaths, being mad, glorious and fabulous all at once.

Incase you need the reminder...

The Wild Donkey wants you to:

FINISH IT.

Don't hold it up.

Don't wait for the perfect creative time.

Don't wait for anyone else.

Don't wait for a publishing deal.

Don't wait for outside validation.

Create it until it's done, then RELEASE IT.

Jump on the wave of inspiration, and surf it out it until the wave is done.

You don't need to be properly prepared.

You just need to do your job.

RIDE ZE WILD DONKEY!

Do it. Create it. *Have faith in it.* Finish it. Release it.

Go grab your cowgirl hat!

Youcandooooeeeeeeeet!

Artist Goddess

She brings colour &
joy into the world.
With ink, pen, brush,
paint, glue, paper
she creates the
world anew.
Magic ~~the~~ flows
through her hands,
changing everything
she touches into
a miracle: a rainbow
artwork of the
soul. She is an
artist
goddess...

©leonie

Who is a Creative Goddess?

A little while ago I did a profile interview at my cubicle job – which basically entails me walking around talking to interesting people and writing about it. Anyway – one day I was talking to a guy, and I asked my trademark question. "So, what makes you awesome?" And this lovely guy grinned shyly, and said: "I do paintings."

And in my usual, calm, graceful way, I *shrieked*: "That's GREAT! I love it! Tell me more more MORE, you artist you!"

And he backpedalled. "Oh but I'm not an artist or anything! I haven't SOLD anything you know. I just do paintings."

Since when was ARTIST ever about being an occupation, not what we are in our deepest soul?

We were each born artists. When we were kids, fingerpainting gloriously, and someone told us "Oh! Look at you, you artist you!" we would just nod. And smile. Because that's who we were. We just made art because it was fun and it made us happy in our hearts.

When did we decide the only person who could ever call themselves an artist was the one who painted full time as their source of income, sold their artwork and galleries, painted their *fine art* on an easel with nice brushes and did it in an internationally recognised style?

The only person who can ever truly call themselves is an artist needs only one requirement:

They were born.

The tyranny.

Of art needing to Look Good in order to be ART. Or be sold. Or be wildly popular. Or shown in an art gallery.

I don't want to count the times I hear:

"I made this artwork. It was incredibly freeing and therapeutic for my soul."

At which point I'm going YAY! That is perfect! YES! That is true! And then I hear a moment... and then they discount their own art and sacred experience.

"But it doesn't look good. And it won't ever be in a gallery. I'm not an artist or anything!" And even: *"But then someone looked at it and said 'Don't give up your day job."*

(I wish to have a petition against that sentence to refrain anyone from ever, ever saying it again. "Don't give up your day job" – ARGH! What would be a good response to this? "Well, don't give up your day job to have fun, be wild, laugh like a kid again or follow your dreams either then!")

Looking Good and Being Successful and Making Money. That's not the point or value of art. Ever.

The point of art is being freeing and therapeutic for the soul. The value of art is that it serves us, our souls and our dreams in a thousand miracle, rainbow ways.

The point of art is to create it, to let this amazing river of spirit and ideas and texture and colour and imaging flow through you.

The point of art is to feel like a Creative Goddess while you do it.

That's the only point there is.

It's the one that matters.

The Creative Goddess Manifesto

Creative Goddesses make art because it fills them up with joy and light. Creative Goddesses believe mistakes are sacred and add to an artwork's story and perfection. Creative Goddesses aren't afraid of making art that doesn't Look Good. Creative Goddesses don't make art for others, they make art for themselves. Creative Goddesses make art that is true for them. Creative Goddesses don't need no stinkin' outside approval. Creative Goddesses make art that doesn't need to look like anyone else's. Creative Goddesses trust in their intuition and vision to make *their* art as it is needed in this world. Creative Goddesses listen to their soul's calling. Creative Goddesses dip their fingers in paint. Creative Goddesses know the power of soulful creativity. Creative Goddesses remember that every person on this planet is an artist, a Creative spirit, a soul who needs love, joy, creativity, laughter and connection just as much as water and food. Creative Goddesses do it messy. And gladly. And reverently. Creative Goddesses share their art when it is right for them, and hold on to the medicine of their art when it is right for them.

The Creative Goddess is inside you.

THE SACRED HEALING SPACE OF LOVE

This page is imbued with magical love & healing powers. It will take your words gently & transform them.

What would you like to forgive yourself for?

I've been forming this for a couple of months now, jotting it down piece by piece on scraps of paper, in my journal, in emails to friends. Little reminders for when I forgot or lost my way. Those tiny moments I couldn't find the faith for myself or my dreams, or I didn't know where to head on my path. I wanted to write this for myself, for what I needed to hear from myself. And now I want to share it with you, for all the artists, writers, photographers, mamas, healers creators, spiritual dreamers, poets, musicians & magic-makers who might need some affirmation, some praise, some loving words. We all go to that place of fear. What's important is finding the feet & the path to travel to the next place.

10 Ways To Fly Beyond Creative Dream Frustrations & Fears

1. Let's play a little game I like to call Poignant Perspective.

Inside you, there is a whole world of brilliance and beauty. Imagine the incredible inner terrain that is you: the great oceans of love, the mountains of achievements small and massive already made, the fields of wildflowers singing your name, the rose gardens dedicated to you in your honour.
This whole big amazing world inside you. Try not to focus all of your attention on the little overgrow lot that needs some tending to. Remember, there is a whole world of rainbow beauty inside you.

2. Write yourself an ancient love letter.

Imagine you have long, silky grey hair, wispy, in a braid. In your eyes, there sparkles a kind of wisdom, joy and compassion that can only be found after eighty years on this dear planet. Imagine this precious part of your self, remembering you as you were, smiling gently, sending you love back across the distance. Let this graceful, gorgeous Grand-Mother guide your hand, and write you a letter of all the things you need to know & remember.

3. Comparing is So Last Millenium Baby

Dearheart, you were born on one special moment, one incredible day, one amazing year. Nobody knows the breaths you have taken, all the steps of your journey you have taken since the first. Yes, you are the rarest mosaic of all – a rich & incandescent tapestry enwoven with all the love, lessons & life only you can know & share. Rare tapestries are not meant to be compared in a flea-market-of-the-soul dearheart, and neither are you.

4. Trust in the Universe

Baby, it's got a big & beautiful plan for you so majestic & wide that you can't even dream it right now. Trust. All will be well. You are loved. All will be well.

5. Expand your vision of reality

Those five words have been swimming about in my head for a while now, reminding me:
Expand. E x p a n d . E x p a n d.
Expand your vision of what is possible. What is not true for you, is true for others, and it can be yours if you want it.
Sit in silence, and feel the parameters of your brain. Take a deep breath in, and widen the space your mind inhabits. Widen and expand until you know that what you desire is absolutely, unequivocally possible. Inhabit a new world of Possibility.

6. Check-in at the Creative Dream Lost Baggage Counter

Use the moment of blah, of blankness, of silence to check-in with your creative dream. Is it exactly what you want? Is your current dream the truest expression of your gifts?
This is one my love reminds me of often. I'll be telling him how frustrated I am and he'll say simply: "Is this what you really want? Is this what you were born to do? If there was only one thing you could do with the rest of your life, what would it be?"

7. Whose thoughts are the most important?

Are you waiting for the outside world to approve of you or your dream? Does it matter more what others think of you & your dreams, or is it you?
Meditate for 100 breaths.
See what you find inside.

8. A Plan For The Journey Forward

Do a business plan – but not just a business plan. A plan for your greatest soul's desire. A map towards your truest heart's expression & your dream lifestyle.
Plan it. Put it out there in the universe. And find out the path forward, seeing the trail on your newly defined map.

9. Time To Be Held

Hold your dog/cat/bird/animal/mama earth. Let them love you, and remind you of every single way you are perfect.

10. Everything You Need, You Have

Don't take this list as gospel. write your own. Your own divine, wise, brave wisdom is the Gospel for your life.
Inside you is an incredible Goddess, waiting to help you along your way.
What does she want to say to you?
All the answers you need are already inside. Write your very own list of Creative Dream Flight. You are the best expert on you.

You are a Goddess.

What do you want to say to the world?

Write it down now, baby:

How To Get More Things Created by Ignoring Everyone Else

So sweetheart, there's this funny little routine I do. I have a big, blooming idea. I have a wild donkey to ride, a thing to create, a song to sing.

I dream of it at night. Idea storms brew as I tend to my daughter, passing her dropped toys one by one as she baths. So much to make. So many miracles to create.

And just before the glory begins, as I gather my utensils, as I turn towards the open page... there is a moment.

A moment of stillness where I face the task before me. A moment, a gasp of breath, a blush of fear, a wondering of "just how do I create this baby?"

I think to myself:

I'll just go do some research. Go read somebody else's work. I'll go get inspired that way. THEN I'll be ready to do my work. THEN I'll be ready to give this project life. Give this project the chance to take its first breath.

And if I'm not careful, I turn and back away from the precipice of creation.

I run away in every other direction. To see what others are doing. To compare myself, needlessly. To pin the dream of my idea up against the fully formed flesh of other's projects made real.

And all too often – the energy that's culminated? The idea storm? That wild donkey of mine?

It sifts and silts away. Untended and unadored, it slips from my paddock. It becomes losts in the wilds of Inspiration Not Created, up the back paddock of What Could Have Been.

I'm writing this as an ode.

We all have a dream inside us. A miracle. Rainbows wanting to be birthed.

And my darling, oh what we need for them is courage. Courage to turn towards the page and not turn away again. Patience and tenacity and a mama's kind of ferocious love for them.

I want to hear your story. I want to know of your essence. I need your gifts in this world.

I write this for me. I write this for the world.

We need your gifts, dearest. Please bring your miracles to life.

Turn away from the email the Facebook the TV the books the distractions.

Turn towards the pure essence that is waiting to be born through you.

It can only be you, dearest.

It can only be you.

Secrets to being a Creative Mama

Carry your ART with you.

Be o.K. with Mess.

Don't "do it all" --> Do MAKE ART!

Involve your Kids

Make it A priority

Form Creative Mama TRIBEs & meet regularly.

Laugh at your paint smears

You ARE DOING A MAGNIFICENT JOB!

Give yourself what you need.

Find ways for everyone's needs to be met.

SACRED GODDESS

Walking the Wise Woman Way

I am pregnant, and I am terrified.

On the outside?

I'm glowing. At peace. The image of a radiant mama to be.

On the inside?

I feel overwrought and anxious that I'm on a train that I can't control.

I'm afraid of birth. I'm afraid of doing it wrong. I'm terrified my sweet babe will never turn from being breech. I'm afraid of never finding any other mamas who understand me. I'm afraid of losing myself.

*

My love sees the way I tear up on the way home from birth classes. How I snap at midwives. How I grieve after reading every painful birth story.

And together, we reach out for help.

We find an acupuncturist who specialises in helping turn Little Breech Mermaids.

He listens to my pulse with his hands, and tells me:

I can feel your stress in your pulse. We will fix this too.

And I believe in him.

*

My love takes me to a Jungian psychotherapist with a large bowl of rose quartz crystals beside her.

She has kind eyes, and reminds us of Nan – our ninety year old elderwoman who listens with kindness.

She tells me stories of calling the angels around a birthing woman, and whispers:

Leonie, you don't have to be normal. You can make your birth and life how you like it.

Do you think, she says, *you could come from your place of power instead? So you don't take things so personally?*

Instead, you'd just be a woman living her truth, joyful again in her own life, doing what she wants to do, being how she wants to be.

And I glimpse that might just be possible.

She had given me the gift of a vision I can walk towards.

*

In the morning, I rise.

Go give thanks to Great Spirit,

says a voice inside me.

I set off for the western mountain near here, walking up it with three incense sticks, hands in my pockets, stopping every few moments to let my belly settle and my back stretch.

At the top of the mountain, there is a wise old tree surrounded by a natural forming stone circle.

I bow my head as I walk up to it, asking the tree, the stone circle, the earth angels if I may enter.

They welcome me.

I ask my guides to be with me.

I step into the circle, and nestle beneath the tree, removing my shoes and leaning my back up against her rough bark.

Immediately, I feel held by her branch arms.

Immediately, I feel surrounded by the ancients, my elders, my teachers.

I want to cry. It is a relief to find them again after feeling oh-so alone.

And here they are, on the mountain, waiting for me to come and speak with them again.

*

I light the three incense sticks of Nag Champa – one for me, one for my love, one for Little Mermaid. Three souls who have chosen each other to walk their journeys with.

I dig the sticks into the earth, let the smoke waft over me.

I let my eyes swim and fade, and I breathe.

I close my eyes until the morning light awakens the spirit in me.

When I open them again, I look out over the valley, over the suburb, the wide green sheep farms leading up to the next mountain range.

Suddenly, the mountains are not ordinary Canberra mountains anymore – I see them light up and gloam like the mountains at home, like the hills of Avalon.

And the mountains weave their magic, and I hear the voice:

*

You are a wise woman, walking your wise woman path Leonie. You must remember this.

You worry that you do not know what to do – that this is your first time. Remember the wise woman way, and remember you have done this before, over and over.

You have learned so many gifts and know so much wisdom and tools from your journey. Use these, now and always.

Motherhood and birthing is not separate from your spiritual journey. Why would you separate them?

You can be a shamaness when you give birth. You can be a wise woman when you mother.

All these things are woven together. You are not alone. When you became pregnant, we did not leave you to experience this life thing. It is not a separate journey from your spiritual path. It is all a part.

We need you to be a wise woman now. We need you to blaze your light on your path ahead.

Women tell you their birth stories filled with pain because they have a wound. They did not know the path of the wise woman way when they birthed. They did not know. We need women to be able to know the *wise woman way if they want it. You can help in bringing this to those who need it.*

But for now, plait your hair and lace feathers through it, like you always have done. Stand on the top of the mountain, staff in hand, and see how the mountains glow.

Remember again this world is filled with light, with spirit, with wisdom, with joy... that birthing and mamahood is a part of this.

We are not asking you to be different from who you are... we are asking you to remember who are you are, deep down in your cells – the woman of power, presence, knowing and radiance.

Bring this into your journey now. You belong here.

*

And I see the future unfold before me. The Leonie who had forgotten she could be a Goddess, and walk her medicine path, even as she birthed and became a mother. The Leonie who remembered the courageous, brave, light-filled soul inside her. The Leonie who knew again that she felt lost when all she needed was to bring her soul's sacred work back into her life.

And I saw that I was meant to be here, right here and now, beneath the sage toned mountains of Canberra. And that one day soon, I would live again beneath the deep blue mountains of Proserpine, the town named after a Goddess, creating our retreat, teaching other women the path of the wise woman too.

*

I'd been worrying about the outcomes of my life and my birth. I was afraid of having a cesarean if Little Mermaid didn't become un-breech. I was terrified of being transferred to the hospital. I was afraid of not reading All The Books beforehand. I was afraid of not applying all the concepts of ecstatic birthing and attachment parenting correctly. I was afraid of not getting breastfeeding right. I was afraid of not knowing all the herbal healing remedies I might need. I was afraid that I might not be calm. I was afraid I might not have prepared hard enough, or meditated long enough before Birthing Day came.

I had a ginormous score card of my performance, and was so ready to judge myself.

And I see that that fear of Getting It All Wrong – it came from that place of feeling lost, alone, and grasping at all straws.

It came from a place that didn't believe that in my cells and in my soul, there lived the wisdom that I needed.

Now I see that my real fear... was losing myself.

As soon as I remembered I could be a wise woman and a goddess, as I birthed and as I became a mama... things began to make sense again.

It didn't matter if I ticked all the boxes anymore. It didn't matter how Little Mermaid chose to come into the world.

It didn't matter what others thought of me.

All that mattered was that I had *me* again... me and the way I choose to walk the path of my life.

I was no longer lost. I was no longer alone.

*

Inside me, there lives a wise woman. She has lived many times before. She shows me the way.

She teaches me the path of courage, healing, joy and knowing.

I place my hand inside hers.

I turn and face the wind.

The light glows warm on my face.

My waxing-moon belly rolls like the ocean, bearing the fruit of a new goddess, and a new life.

My legs are strong. They know this land.

I can be a goddess. I can be a wise woman.

Because that is who I *am*.

Now that I have found my self again,

I am home.

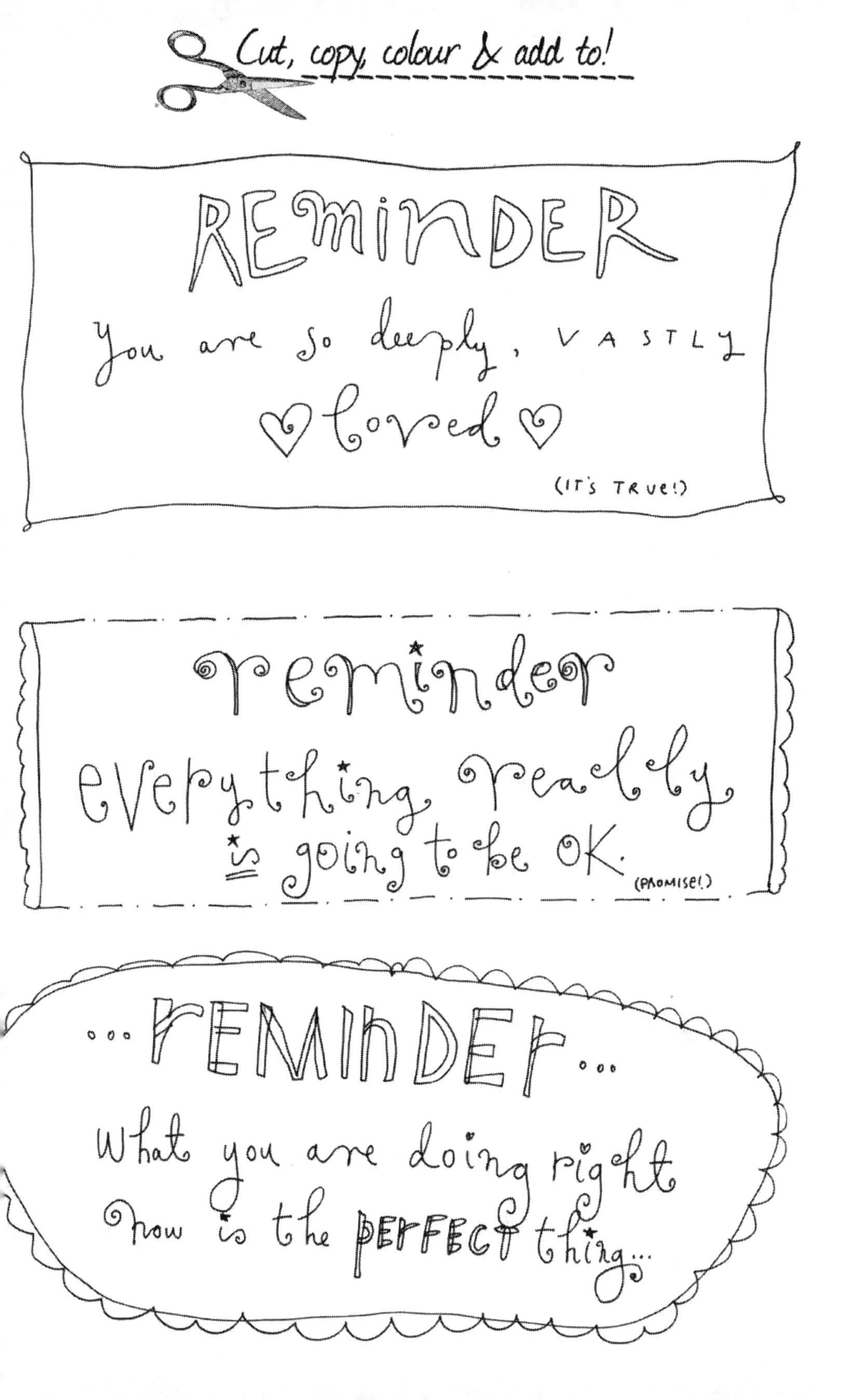
Cut, copy, colour & add to!
REMINDER
You are so deeply, VASTLY loved
(IT'S TRUE!)
reminder
everything really is going to be OK.
(PROMISE!)
...REMINDER...
What you are doing right now is the PERFECT thing...

What are you unique gifts?

What makes you an Earth Angel?

What makes you special?

(start peering into your light!)

How to Develop Your Intuition

I haven't always been intuitive.

It's true. And when I say that, what I really mean is: I haven't always been **aware** of my intuitive gifts. I know we are all born with them, it's just it can take some time to awaken to them and learn how to hear them and trust in them. It's like going through school – a class of Hearing Intuition 101 there, a class of Believing Intuition 202.

Story time

Sometimes, instead of just hearing wisdom and words and trying to apply them... it's easier to understand through stories. We are story people – our world is filled with stories, and they can change how we see the world. They can touch our heart, and awaken new rooms in our soul. Stories are sacred.

The best story I can share about intuition is this:

Once upon a time, a couple of years ago, me and a couple of women sisters had a women's circle one night. We thought we would have one on the top of a hill near the sisters' place. When we got there, we could see a storm coming. We decided it would be far richer to circle in a storm on a hill than just sit inside and do it. So up the hill we climbed, to the rocky ground near a large old tree. Mama Trees arms opened wide, arching into the sky, holding us safely.

It was exquisite.

All around the mountain, we could see the misting rain. It glowed with far-off lightning, and the gold of streetlamps. Every strand of grass moved in the breeze, the rain dripped from our chins, the wind touched every hollow of our cheeks. It seemed the whole earth was alive, reaching up to embrace the rain, tingling with energy. It was wild. Beyond wild. It felt deeply ancestral and ancient to be up there, huddling in a circle of women as the world storm-danced around us.

Finding the words.

As we do in circle, we took a talking stick. And each woman voiced her truth, her soul's story as she held the talking stick. She shared about her life and her journey and all that had been coming up for her. As always, it was perfectly raw and exquisite – to hear women sharing deeply from her heart and spirit is always an honour. The talking stick was passed to me. The wind whirled around us. The night gloamed. The soil had splattered on my ankles.

All of a sudden, I couldn't speak English.

That non-crazy time I-couldn't-speak-English

Inside my mind, I was thinking "But you must speak English! That's what's expected! That's how you communicate! If you don't speak English, what on earth will you speak?" And inside my soul, I could feel this deep, instinctual need to speak another way. I decided to follow it. I wanted to see where it lead. After many soft moments of composing myself, I managed to say (in English):

UP HERE, ON THIS MOUNTAIN, ON THIS NIGHT, I DON'T FEEL LIKE I SHOULD BE SPEAKING ENGLISH. I FEEL LIKE I SHOULD BE LISTENING TO THIS, AND SPEAKING WHAT FEELS REALLY, REALLY RIGHT TO ME RIGHT NOW.

I looked around at my circle sisters. Their eyes were large in the light of the night, and they nodded their understanding.

And so I took a deep breath in, and I listened. And then I began speaking.

It was a language that tasted of earth and life. It bubbled over rocks like a river. It burst like a rain drop on cement. It sounded like leaves rustling, of soft humming, of a woman who listened to herself. I would hear pockets of expression, and I would sound them out, mouthing them out, head cocked to the side, listening. I was simultaneously utterly surprised at what came out and deeply comfortable with them. It continued until it finished.

And we sat there again, the wind and the rain and the night and the light all around us.
Listening, being, feeling wild and wonderful.

Maybe.

Maybe I was remembering part of my ancient self.
Maybe I was speaking the sounds of the earth.
Maybe I was speaking a language from a past life, when I circled with other women on mountains.
Maybe it was all of these.

What I know for sure though is this:
I LISTENED TO AND FOLLOWED THE INTUITION WHEN IT CAME THROUGH.
And that makes all the difference.
All the difference in the world.

What intuition looks like

Sometimes intuition is a tiny calling in the chest.
Sometimes it is a wild little desire to do something.
Sometimes it feels like a big knowing.
Sometimes it feels like a compass in the belly, pointing you in the direction where you need to go.

How to start working with it

Start exploring it. Trying new little ways to explore it and test it. To know when your intuition is coming from your grounded Goddess self, and to know when it is coming from somewhere else.

Up there on that mountain, following that wild calling in me to speak another language awakened another world inside me. I felt I could do anything because I'd **trusted** my intuition, and **followed** it. It was kind of a big way to try it out, but I was in a safe place with trusted friends. Afterwards they remarked just how RIGHT it felt to listen to me speak in another language. Flex your intuition muscle with friends who understand and honour you and your intuition building.

Or try out your intuition muscle in other ways to help you feel safe and honoured. This morning I woke up with a dear friend in my energy. I emailed her and said "Sweetie, I'm not sure if I'm right on or not, but I feel your spirit is feeling sad, and I want to reassure it that all will be well. If you're feeling great though, that's great!" She wrote back to me thanking me for the message and sharing about her spirit sadness. It was a beautiful exchange – and I'm so grateful I listened to my intuition.

See your intuition as a muscle that **is** inside you, it just needs attention and building.

How I share my intuition now...

When I decided or **knew** that I wanted to share my intuition more, I created Goddess Guidance sessions – a blend of Goddess coaching and oracle reading. Every time I go to do one of these sessions I wonder – what if I don't know what to do? And then I place my trust in my intuition – to the spirit inside me. I listen. I trust it. I speak it. And every single time, miracles happen. I finish sessions and wonder how on earth my intuition could know that. And yet it does. I just needed to listen.

What happens if your intuition is wrong?

Sometimes what you think is true doesn't seem to be. There's a couple of reasons this can be the case.

- **Timing**: Your intuition may end up being true – but you only find that out in a month or a year or ten years. It can take time for the universe to unfold.

- **Lost in Spirit's translation**: Sometimes when we hear intuition, we don't fully decipèr the message. Sometimes messages about others can be messages about what they represent inside ourselves – our own sacred mirror. Discerning what is true for us can take time, and it's a beautiful process to learn through.

What matters most...

What matters most is listening and believing and trusting in your intuition.

In seeing where it leads to. In playing, and exploring, and building your intuition muscle.

Inside us there is so much wisdom and knowing...

and it is such a joy to access it, learn it and grow it.

Every morning
she woke up &
tried to find her
way home into
herself...
Some days it
was easy... some
days the path
home was long
& rocky...
but she remembered
to be gentle &
know that all
will be well...

RADIANT GODDESS

Six Ways to Self-Soothe

This is brought to you by my attempts at getting to sleep last night. I was feeling unsettled both physically and emotionally – a touch of heartburn, a little bit of monkey brain and a splash of not-feeling-good-enough. Those sneaky little emotions that can creep up on you when you're tired, and then make it hard to actually get the thing you need – some soul-replenishing sleep.

So I dug through my medicine bag to find what tools might work to self-soothe. And I thought I'd share a list of tools here which you can use in as stand-alones or combinations to find your way home to self-soothed again.

1. Crystals

I keep a bowl of tumbled crystals on my bedside table and use them in some way most nights. Usually I choose one to go beneath my pillow or hold in my hand. Last night when I needed some extra crystal loving, I found three that felt right. I put a rose quartz on my head to help find loving thoughts again. I put an amethyst and a smoky quartz on my neck where it felt like my emotions were stuck. Within a couple of moments, I felt my body start relaxing and began to feel better.

My tips for using crystals: Use your intuition. Select ones that seem to be the right ones. Don't worry too much about book definitions of them. Place them wherever it seems to need it. Keep moving them until it feels right for you, and you feel the energy begin to un-stuck and flow. Crystal energy is powerful and healing and beautiful. They can be an amazing self-soothing companion. See what works for you, and trust your intuition. It will lead you home.

2. Affirmations

Last night, I used the combo of crystals & affirmations to self soothe. After placing the crystals on my head and throat, I made the mental choice to start affirming. I started using affirmations that worked with me: *I am loved. All is well. I am surrounded by love. Today is a wonderful day. I am so blessed. All is working with the divine.*

Once I'd stabilised my inside-views, I turned my attention to my outside-views. Particularly, people who I was worrying about or felt hurt by. On my wall I have a hanging called the Native American Commandments. It's a little tacky, but I bought it for one of the commandments. It says:

Speak the truth, but only of the good in others.

That to me feels like a whole lot of freedom. It can be so easy to put our judgement hats on and make divides between us and other souls. What if we had the freedom to speak our truth, but only of the good in others? We would really need to peer into them to see their beauty, and the real truth of them.

So I shifted my thinking. And my little feelings of worry or fear or pain about people turned to love and accepting as I started numbering the ways they were beautiful. It felt like I was awash with love instead of division.

As always, use affirmations that resonate with you, and that you can believe in.

3. Check your sensitivity levels

At night time, our sensitivities can come out, and show us what we might be consuming that doesn't work for us. This might be movies, books, food or connections that don't help us feel good.

What I noticed when I became vegetarian three years ago was that in the two weeks of detox-ing from meat that I did, I had violent, fear-filled nightmares. Nightmares that I'd always had throughout my life came up, in vivid colour and emotion. It felt like all the pain of meat was leaving my system. After those two weeks, I felt more peaceful and calm than I'd ever before. The nightmares disappeared – where once I had them once a week, I've had them less than a handful of times in the last three years.

In the past couple of months, I started eating little bits of meat. At first it was to boost my iron levels, and then I just kept doing it. I wouldn't call myself full blown carnivorous, but I'm definitely more omnivoric than herbivoric right now. What I've noticed is that I've got that stuck feeling of anxiety, fear and tension again. Not all the time, but it's there. It's the feeling I get from meat.

So right now – I'm noticing that, and seeing what I might to do with that. I don't need to push myself to make a decision – the right one will come when the time is right.

So the meat thing probably contributed to last night. As did the fact that I did something I normally don't do, and watched a movie that was above kids rating. I know that my energy is sensitive, and that action-filled, suspense, horror or any kind of violence REALLY doesn't make me feel happy, safe, calm or blissed out. I think we are all way more sensitive than we give ourselves credit for or take seriously. Anyway, yesterday I watched Grosse Point Blank again. Which is a John Cusack movie (who I think is lovely) and it's basically a romantic comedy, but is about a hitman. Wayyyy more guns and blood and stuff than I ever usually put myself through. And as much as I love the JC, I felt unsettled after watching it. Like "Uck, did I really need to put myself through that again?"

People always say: it's only a movie. Yes, but the idea of a movie is to create a sensory space for you to experience something. And seriously, if we were actually to LIVE the stuff that happens in action-y movies, it would be a huge emotional and physical and psychological tragedy that we'd have to heal. So why would I put myself through the sensory experience of that?

I choose movies and TV and books that make me feel good. That remind me of the highest truth: that anything is possible. That I am loved. That the world is a beautiful, magical place. (Thus my predeliction for kid's movies. Kids have got it so right!) I'm really choosy about what I consume. Our spirits are gentle and want to be nurtured.

So watching a shoot-em-up movie that made me feel really unsettled probably didn't help last night.

And then I read a crappy novel before I went to bed. Again with the choosiness. It didn't contribute to my happy inner or outer-view. I felt as confused and anxious as the characters did. So I'll put that one aside to either not finish reading or not read before sleep – we are at our most sensitive to outside energy then.

So a combination of sensitivities from consumption of books, movies and food didn't help me to feel calm and soothed last night. Which is a beautiful thing, because it reminds me what I need to do to restore calm again. And it reminds me that I'm a sensitive little soul, as we all are on different levels, and I need to be careful of what I show to myself.

4. Calling all angels

Last night I was feeling really anxious and vulnerable. I found myself wanting to cloak myself with a Cloak of Invisibility. As a passionate, intense lil Scorpio, I've learned the art of making myself invisible when I don't want to be seen. I don't think I manage to do it in an insipid-fade-into-the-background kind of way. It's more of an intense kind of energetic-walling. (If you ever want an energetic bridge burned, hire a Scorpio.)

So I've noticed that this is my habit, my pattern, my way of doing life. And last night, I felt that the same desire came up for me again last night. And I felt a pain in my heart and tears in my eyes – I don't want to keep running from my own vulnerability. I don't want to live my life cloaked.

So I really felt this. And I also felt like I still needed some kind of protection. So I wondered what I could use instead of a cloak – and I got the image of big, bright, white angel wings coming from behind me and folding around me, encasing me in a circle of unconditional love. As I went to sleep, I asked for all my angels to be with me, and for one of them to hold me in the safe compass of their wings.

So today, as I went about, I walked knowing I was safe inside the embrace of an angel's wings. It was so deeply comforting, and instead of feeling vulnerable, in pain and energetically lashing out, I felt a soft light of love around me.

And it actually showed. At my office job, a new guy at work stopped me in the kitchen and said "You know you're the light of the floor, right?" It kind of took my breath away – that I was so seen in light when I had been wanting to hide in my shadows.

So call on your angels. Ask them to do what you need in order to feel safe, comforted and soothed. Let them hold you.

5. Making Fun

I'm a big proponent of that most sacred of activities – FUN. There's nothing that makes me feel calmer and more joyful than making some silly fun.

Fun is often the stuff that kids do. Fun is playing. It's being creative. It's canoe-ing. Horse-riding. Picnicking. Having everyday adventures. Doing stuff that you normally don't do.

Today, we made a new Fun Game. Me & my cubicle wonder-friend Artemis decided to do fashion photo-shoots at lunch. In the office. There was crawling under desks. And standing on chairs. And avant-garde urban corporate shots. And then ridunkulous amounts of photo-geeking out.

It was silly, and it was sustenance to my soul.

Fun is vital. I need fun like I need sunshine and water. So it's my number five way of self-soothing.

As my amazing healer friend Donna says "**Laughter and tears are both equally healing.**"

6. Give yourself what you need.

During my life-year I get a couple of special weeks that I call "Big Medicine Week."
Helllloooo buttons getting pressed on every single level! Oh hi exhaustion and needing to retreat! Hi hi waves of emotion! Hola huge big painful sore lessons emerging! Welcome back every fear, inadequacy or pain I haven't fully healed!

It's been a time that I've definitely needed to self-soothe.

And I've needed to do that one thing that I forget to do:

Give myself what I need.

And when I asked myself at first what I needed, I didn't hear anything. And then I heard:

You need to feel this.

So I sat with all those feelings. I didn't try to make them feel better. I didn't squash them down. I didn't resist them. What a change that was – I'm the self-apointed Queen of Having All My Stuff Together.

This week, I needed to not have it all together. This week, I needed to not do so much. This week, I needed picnics and tears and bed and snotty tissues. This week I needed to be vulnerable and tell my love, family and friends how I was feeling. This week, I needed to feel it all, and give myself what I need.

Today is one of my usual work days – usually filled with To Do lists and hyper-business. I spoke with my business accountability partner this morning, and in her usual, beautiful, centred way, she asked me what I needed today. And the answer was this:

Today, I need to lie down in front of the tv, and read, and do a little bit of painting.

And so I am.

Turning up, and giving myself what I need.

What do you need to give yourself right now?

8 Ways to receive a healing from nature

All around us – we have access to the most powerful, loving {and free!} healer.

Whenever you are feeling down, out-of-sorts, out of energy, or in need of recharge... here are eight beautiful ways to receive a healing!

1. Animals

Whether it is your own puppeh or meow – or a free-roaming animal {from caterpillars to birds to butterflies}... animals are a beautiful all-rounder healer. They can heal in a moment with their love and joy – as well as each having their own individual medicine to heal with.

Whenever I'm sick or in pain, my Charlie puppeh will lie himself as close to the place of pain as possible... he is my own little healer intuitive doggy.

2. Moonlight

Sleep in a moonbeam – or just step outside before going to bed to stargaze and bathe in the moonlight for a moment.

Moonlight helps us regulate our hormonal and sleep cycles, awaken our intuition and helps our feminine energy bloom and grow.

3. Sunlight + Wind

If you feel like your energy is old, stale or negative, just pop outside and let the sunlight warm you, and the wind kiss your face.

It will clear away all that excess energy el pronto, and return you home to yourself.

4. Earth

If you feel rundown, depleted or like you are too much in your head with swirling thoughts, head outside.

Place your bare feet and hands on the earth, and it will recircuit and rebalance your energy, and help you feel grounded and whole again.

5. Salt water baths + Ocean

These are beautiful to use when you are detoxing emotionally or physically, or feeling negative.

Both will help cleanse and clear you.

6. Sunrise + Sunset

The gorgeous light at sunrise and sunset clear all your chakras... immensely healing! Just step outside for a few moments at sunrise or sunset to feel all beautiful and balanced again.

7. Trees

Sit beneath a tree, climb one, or lean against one... trees will help ground you, as well as filling you with strength and wisdom.

8. Flowers

Flowers have the most beautiful healing medicine – they work with the fairy kingdom to give light, joyful healings.

Yesterday, I was feeling a little toxic, so I walked around our garden, smelling roses, wafting purple flowers around my aura, and lying down among the cheerful yellow flowers.

Within five minutes? Feeling totally healed again!

Where
do you feel
most at home?

The Smoothie That Will Make You Feel Like a Goddess

What's the VERY best way to start feeling radiant in your body again?

If you just make ONE change in your diet, make it this one – just add in a Goddess Green Smoothie.

It's perfect for:

★ breakfast

★ when you are feeling run down

★ when you know you need more greens in your diet

★ when you are suffering from 3pm-it is.

Blend:

✓ 1 banana

✓ A handful of mixed berries (I buy them frozen)

- ✓ A handful of baby spinach leaves or lettuce leaves

- ✓ A splash of water.

And then add your extra goodies!

I add into mine:

A teaspoon of Maca Powder

This tastes to me like burnt vanilla. It is a ground up Andean root vegetable, and chock-full-o nutrients. For me, Maca has helped me even out my moon cycles of bleeding {before I became pregnacious}, recircuits my nervous system and gives me a beautiful, grounded burst of energy. Maca can also help with boosting sex drive, fertility, helping balance all your organs, and soothing anxiety. As with all herbs, I totally suggest trying it out, and seeing if it seems to sing and resonate with you. I know Maca really, really works with my body – it may or may not for yours.

Two Spirulina tablets

Spirulina is a super green food, and is made from a microscopic freshwater plant. It is brimming with antioxidants and iron and good bits.

Go with whatever superfoods or extra nutrients you like... or stick with the plain green smoothie... it's all good.

If you want it sweeter:

Add some agave nectar, maple syrup, stevia or some dates into the blender as well.

The most important thing:

Try it out – make it as simple and as delicious as you want it to be.

Goddess Green Smoothies are the most incredible way I know of feeling radiant again.

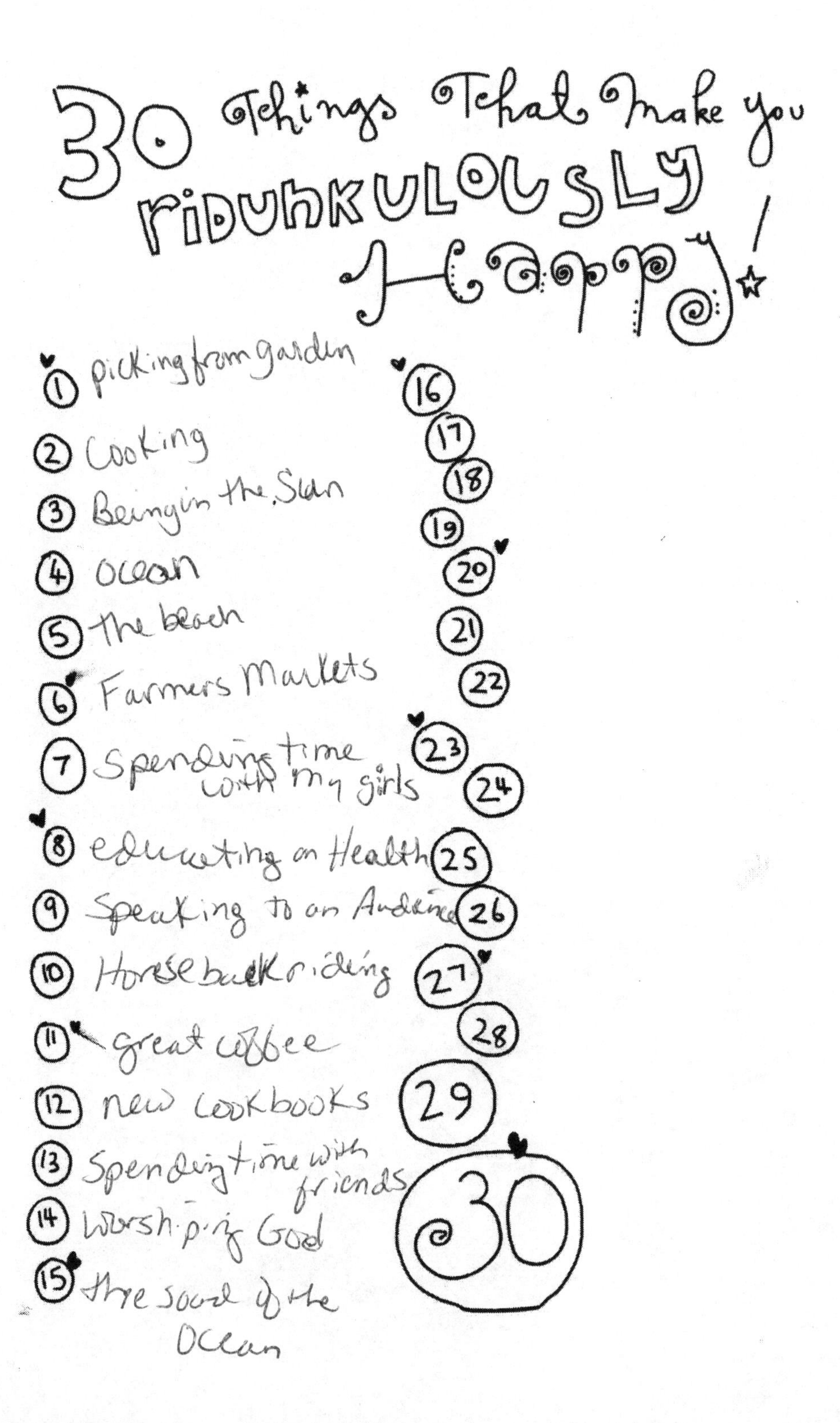

30 Things That Make You
RIDUHKULOUSLY
Happy!
1 picking from garden
2 Cooking
3 Being in the Sun
4 ocean
5 The beach
6 Farmers Markets
7 Spending time with my girls
8 educating on Health
9 Speaking to an Audience
10 Horseback riding
11 great coffee
12 new cookbooks
13 Spending time with friends
14 Worshiping God
15 the sound of the Ocean
16
17
18
19
20
21
22
23
24
25
26
27
28
29
30

Sacred Cave Time

AAs women, and as souls, wherever we are on our journeys – we all need Cave Time.

First of all... what is cave time?

When I was a kid, I did a whole lot of cave time – I'd go out into the world to go to school, then come back home and need some solitude to get back to my core again.

I was a bit of a sensitive kidling {as I think we mostly all are} – I didn't really enjoy too many outside connections, found it hard to make friends (I just wasn't that interested) and would feel overstimulated when I wasn't at home. I needed some of my own cave time at home everyday.

My cave time meant reading piles of fiction books (Enid Blyton, Roald Dahl) , sitting in trees and spending a lot of time with my German Shepherd best friend Clancy, and my horses Dawn & Rebble.

When I went to boarding school when I was 16, I was in a dormitory of 20 other girls – we didn't have rooms, we had dividers. Holy energy overload batman! I found cave time again by making my own little divided space a sanctuary of my own artwork, photographs, quotes and beautiful things. I'd escape back home to the farm whenever I could to eat hot bread with mum, sleep and be out amongst nature again, away from everyone else. It was like coming back home to myself.

I didn't have a name for what I was doing – I just did it instinctually.

The Medicine Wheel

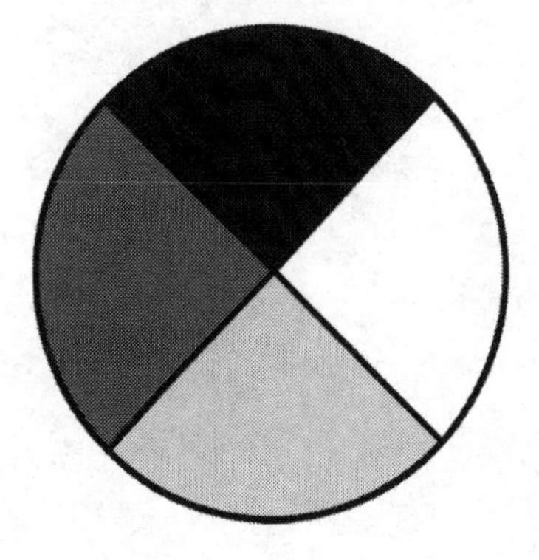

I first heard the words "cave time" in my first women's circles. Finally – a name for that Thing I Knew. In the Native American spiritual tradition, the Medicine Wheel teaches us the four directions of life.

North – the place of earth – where we learn to walk our talk out in the world, supported by our ancestors.

East – the place of air – where the new day is born. It is the place of inspiration and new ideas.

South – the place of fire – the place of passion, energy, fertility. The hot summer of the wheel.

West – the place of sea – the place of introspection.

With each circle of the medicine wheel – where we walk our talk, gather new ideas and bring them to fruition, we return to the West, to go into our caves.

When you know it's time to go to the Cave

Once I learned the teachings of the Medicine Wheel, those feelings & knowings that had always been inside me made sense. And as I began walking the Medicine Wheel within those circles, I learned how each direction felt. I'm a soul who loves to share and be out in the world, connecting & gaining inspiration. But after a while, my spirit begins to feel as though it has been out in the sun for too long. A little bit of soul sunburn maybe?

How do you know when it's time to go to the cave?

You might have feelings of rawness, or soul sunburn. You might be taking on too much of other people's energy/story/worries. You might feel like you've forgotten your soul's own song and that you've been listening to others too much. You might feel exhausted and depleted, with nothing left to give to others or yourself. You know you've reached Cave Time when all you want to do is pull the blanket over your head, and hide out in bed for a while.

When I have those feelings of soul sunburn, I know it is time to gather my bundle, and head West again... to find my cave, to sit in silence, to be introspective, and feed myself first.

Then... when the time is right, and I feel restored in my soul, I feel the callings to walk North again. After time in the West, North feels like remembering how to walk my talk and stay in my own spirit.

How can you do cave time?

Cave time is a way of honouring your body and soul's need to not be "out there" in the world permanently – and a way of remembering your own spirit, essence and wisdom. I'm not a girl who does 100% retreats – the idea appeals to me, but if I waited for the time/energy/opportunity to do a silent, solitary retreat for three days, it just wouldn't happen.

Instead, I do cave time intuitively, instinctually and as simply as I can. Usually it involves not answering calls, taking a few days away from answering emails, not doing any "shoulds", staying at home, not reading websites and just being quiet.

Here's some ways you can "do" cave time:

- ★ Give yourself a break from answering phone calls. Or let the phone go to answering machine, and only pick up if you really want to talk.
- ★ Put an autoresponder on your email explaining you are on retreat and will answer emails in a week (or however long you need).
- ★ Only watch TV that you know will be nourishing to you – watch inspiring documentaries, hilarious comedies or spiritual movies.
- ★ Stop reading other people's websites. This is a big one. Stay in your own energy for a while.
- ★ Have a total media break.
- ★ Book in HOLIDAY on your calendar for at least a day. This means you can't schedule anything in on those days.
- ★ Baths. Quiet time. Sitting in the sun. Meditation.
- ★ Feel free to not contact anyone at all. Maybe you'll still want to contact your small circle of friends. Maybe there will be a circle of people you don't want to contact at all. Honour what you need.
- ★ Read, write, journal, paint – but not for outside consumption. Just for you.
- ★ Give yourself a big permission slip to not care what other people think or feel right now.
- ★ Have what my love likes to call "LBWs" (Lazy Bastard Weekends). LBWs are sumptuous and fun. The rules: *Do only what is lazy.*

Making Cave Time a cycle for you

I forgot about Cave Time earlier this year and had the suckiest of burnouts.

And then I remembered: *There are four directions. Instinctually, I need to honour that a quarter of my time needs to be spent in varying degrees to the West.*

How I make this a reality is that every month, I have a week where I don't take appointments. I go to my cubicle job, but I don't make a crazy to-do list outside of that. I don't do coaching calls that week, and I don't do too much work that requires me to give out too much energy into the world. I just get to sit and breathe and look at my journey from the safety, gentleness and protection of my cave again.

Here's some ways you can make Cave Time part of your cycle:

- Spend some or all of Sunday switched off from being online on weeks that you can.
- Make Cave Time a priority. Repeat after me: *Burnout sucks. I will not go there.*
- Have a "LBW" at the turn of each season.
- Look at your schedule. Can you somehow incorporate some cave time for 25% of your time – a day and a bit each week, or a week each month?

Cut, copy, colour & add to!

Reminder...

You do not need to be anyone but YOU.

You is the perfect thing. ♡

REMINDER

Angels are holding you right now.

reminder

I BELIEVE IN you

When you walk a

SACRED LABYRINTH

You receive jewels of understanding, enlightenment & wisdom. Let your fingers walk this labyrinth. Then write or draw in what you'd like to receive.....

De·Worry Time
THIS IS A JAR. A JAR THAT GOD WILL TAKE CARE OF. ALL those THINGS THAT ARE WORRYING you? Write them on the slips of paper. Hand them over for the angels to hold & take care of
Angel Jar

How To Meditate – For Lazy People

I suspect I'm not the only one in this -
I know meditating is good for me, and yet I don't do it.

I'm not particularly lazy. In fact, I'm kind of a go-getter. I just don't get around to meditating often. I know it's helpful. I know it's good for me. It's also annoying some times, boring at other times and another thing on my too-big to-do list.

And I'm pretty sure I'm not the only one on this.

It's not that we're lazy. **It's just that we haven't found the right way of doing it yet.**

Here's some ways to make meditation less annoying and more like a thing you might want to do.

Get dang comfortable

I started looking at things that annoyed me about meditation - the stuff that held me back from doing it.

And one of the annoying things was this:

I DON'T LIKE BEING UNCOMFORTABLE.

I don't think anyone does. And sitting cross-legged in lotus with a straight back and poised mudra fingers doesn't spell comfortable to me. It spells pins and needles, sore butt and achy back. Maybe when I'm a woo-woo yoga guru master it won't, but for right now, I'm not and it does.

So for me, it's an exercise in getting comfy without falling asleep.

What this looks like to me is a comfy armchair inside, sunlounger on the back deck or leaning against a wall outside.

What comfy looks like to you might be totally different.

The lesson here is: MEDITATING ISN'T AN EXERCISE IN FEELING UNCOMFORTABLE. IT'S A PLACE OF REST, STILLNESS AND COMFORT FOR YOURSELF. GET COMFY.

Leonie's What Works For Me Meditation

I've read books upon books on how to meditate. I have gone to so many meditation retreats and classes it's not funny. I know the meditation routines. I know the old staring at a candle flame one. I know the stilling your mind thing. I know the nose-breathing-in-and-out thing. I know about making your own visualisation.

I also know that they feel like work (blerk). They feel like something I have to work at. It feels hard.
So this is my super-simple-and-not-so-secret way of meditating:

I take 100 breaths. I count them. I try not to think about anything else.

Yup. It's revolutionary.

And it also really works for me. It gives my brain something to do (wee! counting!) while the rest of me is just hanging out, inadvertently meditating.

The lesson here is: THERE ARE SO MANY WAYS YOU CAN MEDITATE. EXPLORE THEM TO FIND A WAY THAT'S REALLY REALLY EASY FOR YOU, AND JUST DO THAT.

The Meditationap

Careful. This one is complex.

Oh yes. It's the love child of a meditation and a nap.

1. Lie down on a bed, couch, sunlounger, or pile your (empty) bath with pillows and blankets.
2. Close your eyes and do nothing.
3. Maybe you'll fall asleep. Maybe you'll have zen inspiration. Maybe you'll just happily float along. Either way, it will be SUBLIME...

My favourite meditationap consists of a sunlounger, a blanket, an afternoon and my ipod filled with lovely music. If ten day zen master meditation retreats consisted of this kind of meditating, I could totally do them!

Penelope's alarm clock

If 100 breaths isn't going to cut it for you, try what works for my friend Penelope. She sets a timer for 15 minutes. She meditates until the timer goes off. This way, she doesn't have to wonder about how long it's been, or how much longer she should meditate for. It's like meditation on cruise-drive.

The lesson here is: MAKE YOUR MEDITATION AS CRUISE-DRIVEY AS POSSIBLE.

Faking it for ten breaths

When I really, really need to meditate, and I don't feel like I have time, I make a little pact with myself. I say to myself:

OKAY, WE SO DON'T HAVE TO MEDITATE FOR ANY PAIN-IN-THE-ASS TIME AT ALL. LET'S JUST DO TEN BREATHS.

And my logic brain says:

TEN BREATHS? YOU THINK I HAVE TIME FOR TEN BREATHS OF MEDITATION? ARE YOU KIDDING ME! I HAVE STUFF TO DO LADY! WE'RE NOT ON RETREAT YOU HIPPY!

And I say:

OH. I KNOW YOU'RE REALLY BUSY. I REALLY FEEL LIKE I NEED THIS. YOU AND ME. BESIDES, IT'S ONLY FOR TEN BREATHS.

Logic brain:

FINE. BUT ONLY TEN. AND I'M COUNTING.

And then we do our ten breaths and it's nice. And we either stop there because we feel like we've refreshed just enough, or we keep going for another ten or twenty because it just feels so good.

The lesson here is: START WITH TEN. EVERYONE HAS TIME FOR TEN BREATHS. SEE WHAT HAPPENS. IT'S A LITTLE WAY OF MOVING AROUND RESISTANCES.

Making it a reward

Meditation should be fun and easy and feel good for you. Not excruciatingly boring or painful. Work out the thing about meditation that makes it really, really useful for you. Not a "I should meditate because everyone says so." Not even an "I should meditate."

Find a way that makes you think "I want to meditate."

Here's the meditation pay-off for me:

Whenever I take 100 breaths, it's kind of boring for the first 59. But then I hit 60, and for the next ten seconds, it feels like nirvana. I don't know if it's a rush of oxygen to the head, or just because I finally relax then, but whatever it is, 60 is good. And it makes those 59 seconds before it so very, very worth it.

My little reward is my 60-second mind orgasm. Maybe I should call it a masm.

The lesson is: FIND YOUR PERSONAL COOKIE-TREAT FROM MEDITATING. AND KEEP REMEMBERING IT. USE IT AS A REWARD FOR GETTING YOURSELF THERE.

Help from guides

When I need extra help in meditating, I use CDs. They are like my own little personal guides into sweet-calm-space.

Try out different CDs, guides, and meditation techniques and see what works for you. And what works for you – make that the golden wisdom in your life. You are the best expert on you.

Here's some different resources you can try out:

* **My Divine Dreaming Meditation Kit.** You don't have to use this meditation to get to sleep – you can use it for 21 minutes of pure, rested bliss. Amen to that! Just head to www.LeonieDawson.com for a copy.

* **Doreen Virtue's Chakra Clearing Book & CD.** I can always recommend Doreen's work. This book and CD is beautiful, easy to use, and the CD meditation is lovely.

The big lesson here is...

The big, big thing I want to share with you from the post is this:

THE REASON YOU AREN'T MEDITATING RIGHT NOW IS NOT BECAUSE YOU ARE LAZY. IT'S BECAUSE YOU HAVEN'T FOUND A WAY TO MEDITATE FOR YOU THAT IS FUN, EASY AND COMFORTABLE FOR YOU YET.

Find the way that does & it's much easier.

Remove the annoying things from meditating. Try out all the different ways, resources and support you can find to make it as lovely an experience for you as possible.

And remember – you are the expert on you. Find the wonderful things that work for you, and ignore the rest.

There are 6 billion paths to bliss, and your path is your own. Make it a happy one.

Meditation for grounding

Go outside. Touch the Earth with your bare hands & feet. Breathe deeply. Breathe in, visualising that you are breathing in through the soles of your feet. Breathe out, exhaling through the palms of your hands. Release anything you wish to let go of by breathing it out. Inhale cleansed, healing light until you feel balanced, whole & connected with the Earth. Stand & raise your arms & breathe deeply. You are a sacred tree: your branch arms in the sky, your legs rooted into the soil. You are the perfect balance between Heaven & Earth.

You only need ten minutes to feel like a Goddess.

Download yours now at:

www.LeonieDawson.com/goodies

MAMA GODDESS

Dear Daughter

Dear daughter of my heart, six-months-old-in-my-womb,

We have three more moons together, where you will be living in my womb, and we are only cells apart.

On July 7th, you came into this world, thirty years to the day that your grandmama & grandpapa pledged their love to each other.

And in a thousand, myriad, rainbow ways, you have changed me, you have changed your papa, and you have changed those who love us.

You feel like sunshine and starlight and laughter and music.

You sing of intuition and mermaids and Atlantis and ancient wisdom and goodness.

You make me believe all the more in miracles, in love, and what we are each here for...

to be the very best part of ourselves.

And you my darling... when you came into my world, I was cleansed clean...

and I glimpse within myself more lightness, truth, love and clarity than I had before.

And it's apparent in my body.

For the first five weeks, I spent my days throwing up, staring at my hands, and trying not to throw up.

I threw up a whole world.

And it was the hardest thing I've ever been through, but I see now what a gift it was.

You cleansed me clean. Every part that needed to be let go of was released.

The oldest of energies was thrown up in our garden, over and over again.

And in the place where I threw up?

Poppies & sunflowers now bloom.

And I feel stronger, lighter and more present in my body than I have in my life.

Without even trying – without any conscious thought or will involved at all – I see my body transforming into the body it was singing to be.

My body – the body I share with you – now moves & eats entirely according to intuition. Some days, all I can eat is the lightest of foods, and think nothing of consuming a bowl of cherries for dinner. Some days, I wake up ravenous for food. Some days we need to cycle. Some days, we need to walk by the river. Some days, we need to swim.

And it might seem like a small thing – but it feels like something much, much bigger is happening here.

I am moulding into the goddess I have always been, the goddess I was born to be, your mama goddess, a creatrix goddess, a loving goddess.

I am strong and courageous... and I am *light*.

You have been a dream come true. I am becoming the woman I need to be in order to be your mama.

Your grandmama said to me at the beginning of all of this:

When I became a mama, I became who I was meant to be.

And I know what she means now.

I know in a way that is in my soul, and in my cells... and the truth of it will continue to be born.

I don't want to say that I can't wait to meet you...

because I've already met you, and right now, we are as close as two bodies could be.

I hold you, and you hold me.

As excited and joyful as I am about your birth, I don't want to wish away these next three moons with you.

Together, we will adventure, and we will laugh.

There will be early mornings where we sit, meditating in the soft dawn light, smiling together.

There will be more naps like this afternoon, where I slept with my belly curled around your daddy's head so we could both feel you move.

Each part of this journey is sacred, and a divine, loving blessing.

Last night, me & your papa were laughing as we watched you flip, over & over in my belly, coming to rest with your back against the left of my belly button.

And your daddy got his big warm hands and softly massaged you through my skin...

and you shimmered, and I felt your joy radiate up to me,

and we watched as you pushed out against my skin, reaching up to touch your daddy.

I will teach you all the beauty, love, goodness & possibility I know in this world.

And I know you will teach me too.

Because that's our sacred contract. That's what we come into our lives to do...

to teach each other, and love each other,

and see God in each other.

That is how it has always been, and how it will always be.

You are a light in our hearts, dearest daughter. We are so blessed to have you in our world.

We will always love you from the stars, and beyond.

I always say:

You were born magnificent.

But I see now that we are magnificent before then too. We come ready made magnificent – even before we are the smallest light of cell... we are already magnificent.

I love you forever,
Mama

She was filled with great excitement at the journey that lay before her.

She did not know how things would be, or how it would change her, but she knew her heart would expand & grow into places she could not yet even dream of....

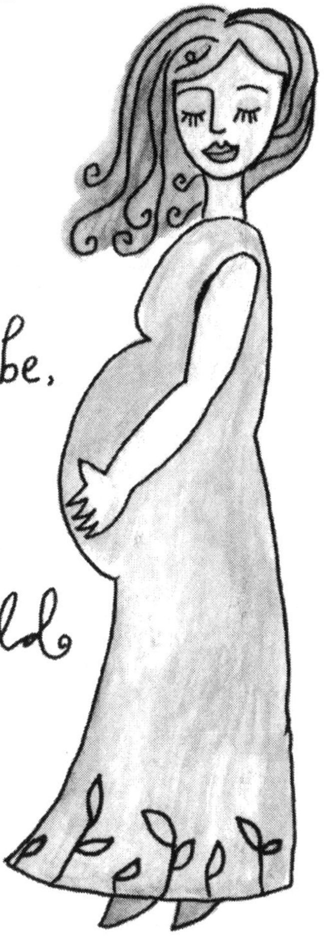

Ostara's Birth Story

An hour before my waters broke.
Photo by Soul Harmony Photography

Dearest Ostara

Where do I begin the story of how you came into the world?

Do I begin when I was sixteen, and saw you as I stood in the shower: a beautiful, wide blue eyed angel with golden curls? I bent down in that shower that day, I bent down before that strong, shimmering vision of you, and I cried, and I laughed, and I knew that one day you would be my daughter.

Do I begin when I was twenty-five, sitting next to your daddy at a spiritual church, and the teacher's amber eyes fixed on us? You have a girl spirit waiting to come through, she said. A daughter. Yes, yes, I know, I smiled back.

Do I begin the story the teary-eyed moment your daddy and I knew you were waiting to come into this world, and we decided it was time? Or the moment I saw those two blue lines on the pregnancy stick, and tears sprung to my eyes? I had only one thought then: *She has come for me. My daughter is here.*

And now, sitting here in the month of April, I write this with you, my daughter, sleeping in my lap. You are three weeks and one day old, and I have been studying your face. You are changing so much already, my beautiful heart. Your round cheeks are lengthening out into your mama's chin. Your eyes are growing a lighter blue. Your hair is becoming lighter and longer.

Each moment, only once.

So my daughter, how do I tell the story of how it is you made the journey from my womb into the world?

It seems too big and too large to write about – there are a thousand threads that weave this story, each string shining, each layer its own song, with flecks of miracles interwoven.

I can only say for sure that I know that you were born exactly how you were supposed to be.

The time had come.
I was kneeling on a hospital bed.
There was only the push.
I was exalted. Strong. Powerful.

After a labour that had washed me off my feet, where all I could do was breathe and keep watching the eternity behind my eyes... this.
Suddenly. It was easy. It was powerful. The push. There was no pain, just the push.

To all other's eyes, I was the sitting sentinel. Throughout the preceding ten hours of labour, I had not moved, not spoken, not even opened my eyes or mouth to speak. I was meditating. I was CalmBirthing. I was the Birthing Buddha.
Inside me though, another story was being told.

I had been walking through the Land Of Birth. I was shamaness. Warrior. I walked deep into caves to fight the Bears Of The Pain Tribe. I had won. My fight had been victorious. I had found her. I was returning home. I was bringing my daughter back with me.

It was early evening. Twilight was soft. There were only small, golden lights on.

I could feel head, shoulders, back, elbows, legs, moving through my hips.

For the first time since I had ventured into Birth Land, I begin to make a sound. A long, deep hymn, a song known only to whales beneath deep oceans and moonlight. My birth song.

There are people all around me in Room Seven. A woman doctor who watched from the corner. Our midwife. Another midwife whose amber wild hair and eyes reminded me of Hera. My love beside me. Our doula. My spiritual mentor.

All around the world, there are people praying. There are medicine men on mountains. Shamanesses burn sage. A tribe of women and goddesses circle, waiting for news. Ancestors and elders from the rainbow world reach out, love touching love, offering a new spirit into this world.

The One That Is Coming? Oh, how loved she is already. We are protected. I know this.

There is only this moment. The moment of push.

Around the hospital, it is A Night Of Birth. Every room at the inn is taken, every manger is being filled with Jesuses, every woman is becoming Mother Mary.

A woman is giving birth in the room next to me. We sing our birth song together.

I sing to her:
"You are strong. You are doing it! You can do it! I am here. We are going to do this. Yes."

I hear her strength song, her own words whispered back to me.
We met each other at the edge of Birth Land, our children in our arms.

Before us, a long, slippery slope down back into the Land of the Others, the Real World.

We look at each other. Our brows are furrowed, damp with sweat. We bare streaks of blood from our initiation. Our hair is wild and mattered.

But our eyes. Oh, our eyes. They are the most beautiful they have ever been. Exquisite. Filled with light and courage and bravery beyond what is known. We have claimed the treasures of our heart – our children. Oh, had we fought for them. With all the love in our hearts and the sky inside us. Oh, we had won.

We turn to the slope before us.

We laugh at each other, and dive... our war cry of

Mooooooooooooootttthhhhhheeeeerrrrrrrrrrrrr....

This is the moment she arrives.
In one breath, one wave of energy washing over me,
she slips from the world inside me, to the world outside me.
She is here.
She slips into the hands of my love.
He gives her to me.
Her eyes are wide open and blue. She lets out one cry.
She is quiet, and strong, and exquisite.
My own personal Jesus.

She is here.
That was the moment.

The moment my daughter was handed from the stars into the world, and into my arms.

The moment I returned into the world, never to be the same again.

Every moment since then.

The hard. The tear stained. The exhausted. The elated. The throbbing love. The glad heart. The brilliant, blindening changes.

The moments that have widened me. Opened me. Made me less. Made me more.

My darling Ostara Light, one day you too might give birth to your own son or daughter. I want you to know that by hook or by crook, however your child comes in to this world is the way they needed to be born.

You may have a water birth, an induction, a caesarean, an orgasmic birth, an assisted delivery, an active birth, a vaginal birth, an episiotomy, an epidural, an ecstatic birth. And they are all equal dearest, because they are all still the act of birth.

Your babe's birth will be an initiation, and you will emerge the warrior mama goddess they need. You will find strength, courage, grace and faith deep inside you, hidden in mountains and trees.

You can do it, my dearest daughter. I believe in you, and know you are supported and surrounded by thousands of angels.

And that, my darling girl, is how I became a mama, and how you were born.

And I don't know how to adequately describe the day you were born...

but I can only tell you

that it was the most magical thing that ever happened to me.

Thank you for being born, my dearest daughter.
And thank you for choosing me.

All the love in the stars and down here too,
Mama

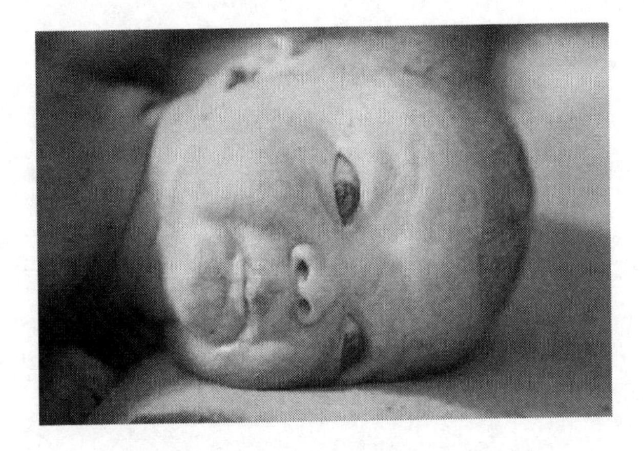

What is your Sacred Birth Story?

(of how you were born or your child)

I am a
goddess

The Best Friend's Guide to Newborns

This was written in the throes of newbornbabyhood, with one hand. It is drenched in tears and milk and a full heart.

I am typing this to you on my iPod with Little Mermaid asleep in my arms. It is 10am, and I haven't slept since 2am, and we haven't had much sleep in the last 48 hours... But here I am, tip tapping you a-way a love letter.

I want to share some of the big lessons and challenges I have found in new mamahood. I can only hope this helps other new mama goddesses out there.

I want to be open with you. Honest. I want to bare my heart to you, so you see me at my most vulnerable & human.

And whisper softly: *Me too.*

People will tell you becoming a parent is hard, and taking care of a newborn is harder. And I didn't really get it, until I found myself sobbing over the bathroom sink at 1am. Some days are easy, and I start feeling like maybe just maybe I have it worked out. On the hard days, I want to run but there is no way I can. On the hard days I tell Chris that as much as I said I wanted four kids, as much as I love Little Mermaid, there is no way I am doing this again. On the hard days, parenting kicks my ass, over and over. **The thing I most want to say to new mamas (and to me) is:** *it's okay to feel this way. You are a good person. You are doing the best you can. And yes, it is enough, and it will be enough.*

Things change every day. You can't really expect much of a pattern. You can hope for it. You can high five your sweet self when lil one sleeps for five hours. But it is probably easier to not expect things to be a certain way. Each moment only once! Some things will work somedays, other days they won't. And that's okay. Keep taking deep breaths and trying new things.

*

As soon as she was born, something was born inside me. **A fierce mama protector bear**. Yesterday my sweetie was carrying Ostara to our car from the shops, looking crazy adorable. I could see all the women around staring at this big bear of a hunk in a grey tee carrying this tiny little pink bundle of baby. As we were walking, we crossed the road (at a crossing). A car drove up, & I wasn't sure it would stop. A calm little thought said in my head "just step between the car and Ostara. That way if it doesn't stop, they will have to get through you before they get her."

And of course the car did stop (as if they would dare take on a big hunk carrying a tiny baby AND a protective bear hippy beside them!) but still... These new thoughts – actually not thoughts – they are INSTINCTS – made me smile.

A mother bear has been born.

Every single mama, father and baby is different. We are all doing the best we can. Let's cultivate a judgment-free zone. I read somewhere this morning (at 3am) that we were the perfect parents until we had children. That made me laugh so hard that I nearly woke up Chris who was trying to get a little sleep for the night. My goodness, I really WAS the perfect parent before I was one. I remember the first time Ostara cried on the second day of her life, and I felt a bit heartbroken... That somehow I couldn't keep her world so pure that she didn't need to cry. That was the moment I started shedding my Perfect Parent Cloak.

*

You get **initiated into a new tribe** when you become parents. You look at other parents like "Ohhhhhhh I get it now! I hear you sister!" Today at the supermarket, Ostara started crying so I picked her up and carried her, and she promptly fell asleep.

So Chris pushed the pram & we used that as a trolley instead, filling it with spinach leaves and bananas and gluten free bread and dog food. And we passed another pram-trolley family, and we grinned at each other, and stopped to coo at each other's bundles, and talk about newborn life.

Instant friends... Something that wouldn't have happened before then.

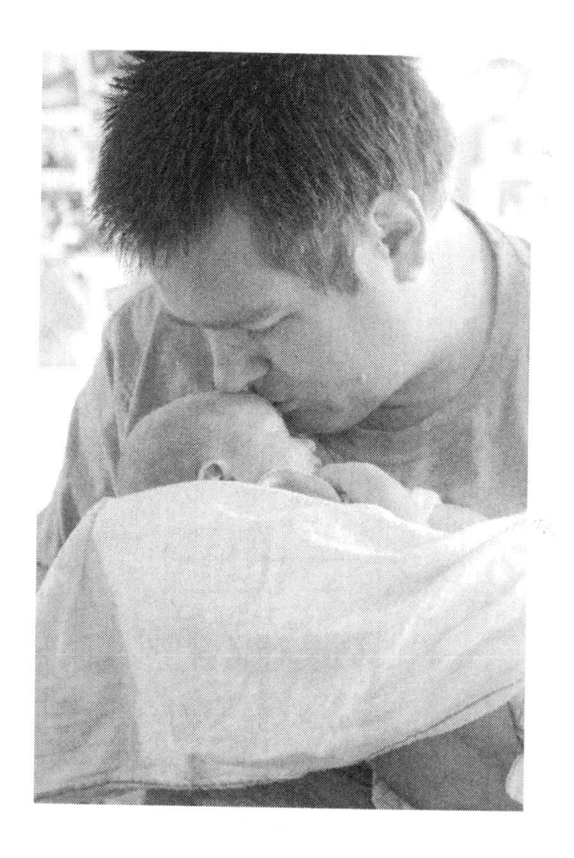

Be good to your partner. Be good to each other. I once read that a baby is like throwing a grenade into a marriage. *Surely not,* I thought. But that's all I could think of as I snipped away at him, tired and cranky. I was so jealous that his life hadn't changed like mine had. That for the most part, I had the lion's share of the caring task what with breastfeeding a zillion hours a day. And I was heartbroken that this was something he couldn't *really, really* understand. He didn't know what mamahood was about – he knew what daddahood was, sure, but mamahood?

I was going through an immense transformation – and the man who is part of every part of my journey, who gets me, who understands everything – he could only look on at the transformation.

I was weary and exhausted and aching to go back to my old life. And I'm sure my love was at times too.

We argued a lot those first few months.

Things got better... but they got harder before they got better, too.

Here's my advice about babies & relationships:

Let go of frustrations as much as you can. Find the gentlest, easiest way possible for you and your love. Parenthood is not a sprint towards perfection. It is a long marathon of love.

And get counselling. Get support when you need it. There's relationship counselling. Or the breastfeeding helpline. There's even authentic parenting coaching by phone. Just anything – anything you can get to support and help you and your love navigate this transformation is a good, needed thing. Everything will be okay, dearest.

*

There is a learning curve to everything.

I thought cloth diapering and baby wearing would be so so easy. Guess what? It came with a massive learning curve and it didn't always work for us.

So I let go of my idea of how perfectly things would work, and got a pram and a box of disposables to support us in the meantime.

The more I get into this mamahood gig, the more I realise that the pram or the no-pram, the cloth or the disposables – it doesn't frigging matter. What matters is what works for you and your family. I really ding dang mean that.

Be gentle sweetness. Do what you can to be gentle with you. These things take time.

Sleep whenever you ding dang can.

Up until Ostara was four or five months old... actually, even longer... I went to bed when she did: 6pm. Because somewhere in that 12 hours of night, I would scrape together enough hours of sleep for it to be enough. I gave up having a night life for a long while. I gave up trying to be a normal person. I went to bed when baby did. I'm convinced it helped me heal from birth and kept me sane and strong when I needed to be.

*

The Four Month Couch Rule.

When you have a babe, pretty much schedule in that you'll be sitting on the couch breastfeeding & holding a baby for four months.

And you'll forget soon after that and think that it really didn't take that long, and when you ask your mum, they'll have no idea that it happened, but yup, it pretty much does.

Breastfeeding takes a ginormous amount of time. It rocks but OMG! The TIME! I remember days when I would be breastfeeding for over 15 hours in a 24 hour period.

I remember attempting to drive 15 minutes in the car, and having to pull over *twice* for breastfeeding top-ups (whether she really needed food or just the comfort of it is beside da point: she wanted *boob*.)

A long, long amount of time is occupied in boob feeding.

Make it as gentle & kind for you as possible. Watch movies! Read books! Buy yourself a Kindle or an iTouch.

Hunky love bought me an iTouch a week or two after she was born when I realised full arms meant no laptop.

And I was really angsty about it, telling him just how much I should be meditating or staring into her eyes or being au naturel for every moment I held her.

Dude, not even the Buddha did that. He just did forty days under a tree! Not four months!

Anyways, my love gently broke it to me:

Honey, I hear what you're saying. But I'd much rather you be sane than be the idea of the perfect parent.

And he was right. As he so very often is.

My little iTouch has been my reading book & radio station & meditation CD player & reach out and connect to the world. I am incredibly grateful for it.

Whatever you can do to make it easy and gentle and happy and sane for yourself during this time is a good good thing.

*

Give your partners the space to become parents.

I ran in the moment she cried in order to settle her. I didn't leave her side for a long, long time. And I criticised the heck out of my partner for not being the exact parent I wanted him to be.

Can I tell you:

It was not helpful to me. It was not helpful to him. It was not helpful to the formation of our little family.

In fact, it sucked a lot.

What helped?

Giving him the time and the space and the opportunity to learn how to settle her himself. And become the Dad he wanted to be. For those two to bond together.

And ding dang, it definitely helped me to have a bit of time and space where I wasn't on duty.

I like what my friend Pixie wrote about this:

"Also, at the very good advice of an elder years ago, I threw my husband to the wolves early on, having to trust he would figure out what to do - which he survived, of course, allowing me to escape the demanding clutches of pudgy fingers now and again. The condition is that I can't critique the job he does if I'm going to claim solitude. It works brilliantly. I don't care if they eat popsicles for every meal and ride the dogs into town bareback. What I do know is that I have to get away and recharge or I will freak the hell out. Letting go gets easier as I practice it."

*

You will heal.

Every week gets easier. Every month gets easier.

You will get stronger. You will find a new way.

Give yourself the support you need. Get help. Talk it out. Be kind and gentle to yourself, dearest heart.

You are doing the hugest job on the planet.

I honour you. I admire you. I am in awe of you. I am stunned at how much love, work, time and energy you pour into your children. You really are incredible.

You are so so so so loved.

You are doing an amazing job.

I believe in you.

I'm sending you all the love from the moon and back... wrapped in the soft arms of Quan Yin to hold you gently.

The Mother I Am

I still remember the nights at 2am. Crying in front of the bathroom mirror, my eyes grey and dark from exhaustion, red rimmed from sobbing.

In the morning, when night broke and left, when light streamed through the windows, when yet another day started, I would search for answers. I had tomes of bibles. All the ways I should be parenting. All the hard, hard lessons I needed to know. There is no test greater than this.

How does one ever prepare for the momentous task of becoming a mother? The answer? One cannot. You only go there. And then you sink and swim, sink and swim. But oh, those tomes. Those bibles. I thought it would be easy. Easy if I did it this way.

Baby would sleep peacefully all day in a sling, and I could continue on with normal life. I could keep creating and sitting and living my magical dream job life. And she'd sleep beside us of course – and that way I wouldn't have to get up all night. I'd barely wake up a bit, you see. And baby and mama would never ever be unhappy, you know... because we'd always be together. Seamless. Unbroken. One organism.

Oh dear, darling me. I look back at my ideas, and I sigh, and I want to hold my young pre-mama self in my arms. I want to tell her it will be different from that. But that it will be okay. We will get through this.

The truth of it is that my little newborn didn't like slings. It was only once she was over 2 months old that it worked for us – before then, she was just too little and squishable. Nor did she like to sleep during the day. And no-way-sies does she then – or now – enjoy sitting. (Consequently, I'm 15kg lighter than I was when I got pregnant. I call it the "Always Moving" workout. And the thing about co-sleeping? For us, I still needed to wake up fully and sit up for an hour every time she wanted to feed every 2 hours. She needed burping and positioning and my pump-action squirtable boobies. It took until she was 3 or 4 months before her little nose didn't get squashed by the Giant Rock Hard Boob as we fed laying down.

Oh and breastfeeding? Yay breastfeeding! But oh the time! Up to 15 hours a day! I remember the days of driving 25 minutes and stopping twice during that time for feeds. And it took until she was six or seven months old until I realised that this mama? This particular constellation of cells? She needs time each day to herself. To sit and create and muse and write and realign her energies. Otherwise she dries up and becomes a parched droughtland of soul. And oh, how she needs to not just survive – she needs to thrive too. This is her holy sacrament – and the lesson that she learned hardest of all.

So here I am. Turning up to you, dearest sister. And being honest. Utterly honest. I want to tell you the good and the bad and everything interwoven. I want to tell you those hard-bound soul truths I have learned along the way. I want to not sugar-coat anything. I want to show you the handful of earth I've scooped up. Together we will see the grit and the glint of gold.

I think back often to those tomes of bibles. The ones which gave me such deep, rich ideas of How It Would Be. They were expectations that I could not live up to. A good book cannot convey all the life that will get in the way.

I used to be fixated on The Mother I Would Become.

Now I'm choosing to cherish on The Mother I Am.

More and more, I am becoming less and less interested in attachment parenting. In continuum concept. In seeking my identity and validation as a mother by medication-free birth, baby-wearing, co-sleeping, breastfeeding, bamboo diapering.

I read all the books while I was pregnant. Before I was pregnant too. I wrapped myself in a haze of:

if I only do this perfectly and differently from how I was raised,
then my baby will be perfect
and she will never suffer
and will never ever go through any pain or discomfort
and all will be right in her world.

(I think that's what all parents hope and want and are afraid of not giving.)

I thought if I securely pushed myself into one tribe, one dichotomy of parenting, then I Would Be Right. That I'd score myself the A+ in the parenting scorecard. I read somewhere that everyone is the perfect parent before they have a baby. And it made me howl with laughter. How true it was for me.

Because I judged. Oh god, how I judged.

I judged the slightest hint of wavering, of humanity in a mother. I judged any attempt by a mother to make it easy on herself. I judged prams like they were little baskets of disconnection.

(And we break for a baby break, as she crawls up to me. I commence singing songs, putting a tshirt on a head like a turban, meandering out with her to talk to her daddy, watching as Ostara is now happy sitting

on one of my paintings, pulling collaged bits off it. I'm happy to sacrifice my painting to the Gods of Babysitting. I take this to be a perfectly excellent distraction for her, run back into my bedroom to continue writing this. This is what it is like to be a mama writer.)

So where were we? Oh yes! The judgment.

Oh my darling, how I judged.

I judged until my insides were pretzalled. I clamored for safety in my judgments. I judged because I thought it made my world safer and more easy to understand. I judged because then I could know the right answer. I judged because then I could say *"If only they ______, their baby would be okay."* As though my judgments would save me, and would save my baby.

Then mamahood came at me like a freight train.

I became a mama, and I tussled and struggled with perfection, with who I was supposed to be and how parenthood was supposed to look.

When babywearing did not work for my infant daughter, I swallowed a large lump of judgment, and brought a pram. And I would walk around with it, wrapped in a cloak of shame and anxiety. I judged myself for every moment she slept in there quite happily, oblivious to the fact that her mama was pushing not only the pram but a train load of guilt too.

I thought if I could just do it perfectly, everything would be right in this world. She would be happy, and wouldn't awake crying. I wouldn't suffer post-natal depression. I would glide into motherhood as easily as a swan takes to water. I would instantly find ease in my long list of attachment parenting and continuum concept requirements.

I would often go through the list of Dr Sear's Seven B's, ticking them off, trying to get each one right. If parenting was a report card, I was scoring myself according to someone else's ideals, not my own.

Can I tell you now that it didn't work?

That it hurt to push myself (and my family) so forcefully into someone else's box? I thought if I sacrificed myself for my daughter every single moment, it would make her life good. It didn't make my life good however – it made me anxious and tight and fighting for breath and sanity and any sense of myself. And that I forgot the one big lesson of my life:

To trust myself.

All my life, I've known that I didn't need to adhere to one faith, one book, one way of being. That all I needed to do was trust myself – trust my intuition – and give myself what I needed. I could survey the spiritual buffet of options, and only take in those things that sang to me, that nourished me, that made me whole.

I forgot I could apply this to parenting.

My report card of parenting would look quite different now.

It would say:

- ★ Baby happy and thriving?
- ★ Mama happy and thriving?
- ★ Daddy happy and thriving?

If no, let's change it.
If yes, then YES! Carry on, dearest!

(Baby has arrived again. She plopped herself upon me, fastened herself to my boob, grown heavier & fallen asleep. I've nestled her into bed, grabbed my laptop, my folder, my large canvas bag that is my Mobile Office, installed my love as the Baby Watcher & walked to the library. The library that was flooded (thanks Cyclone Yasi!) and now smells vaguely of old men and unwashed laundry. But writing time! Oh the glory! My fingers fly across the keyboard as Eva Cassidy plays in my headphones. This is what it is to be a creative mama.)

More and more, I am less convinced that one style of parenting will heal all the wrongs in the world. I am less convinced that The Other styles of parenting will result in adults who are irretrievably damaged. It's all just merging into a blur for me. All it truly means – parenting or religion or *anything else in life for that matter* – is LOVE.

Can I tell you that I know mamas who bottle-feed, breastfeed, co-sleep, have lovely nurseries, are slung, are prammed, have bums in disposables or cotton... and on and on the sameness, the differences, the boring details (because that is truly all they are).

And every single one of them are wonderful, perfect mamas. They have found their own groove. They love their children with all they can – and *they love themselves too.*

Just as I know souls who were raised in a rainbow kaleidoscope of ways... and each of them have their own joys, gladness and lessons. Every single person on this planet can be happy, healed and dancing. However their bum was wrapped. However their heart was held. Whatever parenting books their parents read (or not).

I keep remembering that one of my deepest faiths is this:

Healing miracles can happen in one instant.
Healing and joy is a choice.
And it is up to each of us.

My child will grow. I will love her. I will give her what I can. I will be the mama I am.

I will not give myself away in the battle. More importantly, I will not battle. I will make mistakes. I will feel resentful sometimes. I will open myself to the possibility that love is enough, that healing will part the way – for me, for her, for my love. That we aren't expected to have it all together every moment.

I used to think that I shouldn't have children before *I Had It All Together*. And I thought I did, when I fell pregnant. Then I became a mama. And everything I had together fell apart. And slowly, slowly, I put it back together again.

I don't expect my parents to heal. I don't believe I needed to have a perfect childhood in order to be who I am. Wouldn't that be enormously disenchanting – to know that only our childhood would define the rest of our lives? When what lies within us is an enormous ability to change, learn, grow, shed and transform – all of our own volition. Our lives are not determined by our parents... and yet I thought if I clung tightly to One Style Of Parenting, then my daughter's life would be fine and good and without its own tragedy, medicine and lessons.

But I don't want anyone to take those things from me – I want to live my own lessons. This is mine to live.

My daughter will be who she is. And that is the most exquisite thing I could ever want for her. Any push from me to be the perfect mama is all fallow work. What if I just gave into it? What if I gave up pushing so hard, started resting more, throwing out every book, every judgment, every ideal that I clung to? Where would that leave me? With a tremendous amount of freedom, to feel the way according to my own soul.

I'm not interested in judgment anymore.

I'm longing to return home to that place inside me I have always lived from:

Follow your own intuition.
Be good to yourself.
Joy is an option.
Take from the buffet what is truly yours, and discard the rest – it does not belong to you.

Parenting is one hard bugger of a ride. So overwhelming and frightening that we think – if only I find the *One Thing That Will Make It Allright*, I will prescribe my life to it and not deviate from its plan. But the plan we are meant to be living is our own. The one that makes us all joyful, glad, happy and easy.

I am less interested in ideals anymore. Less interested in deciding what is right in parenting. More interested in finding my own groove, my own style, my own way of dancing this dance of mine. After all – it truly is my own dance.

I used to have this measuring stick of when to accept other people's advice:

Are they happier than me? Does that sound good and true and right to me?

And now I need to apply it to parenting. I will no longer make decisions out of fear, out of tightness. I will make decisions out of freedom, out of lightness and gladness and joy.

So here's my badge, dearest. The badge of how I labelled my parenting style.

I just don't care anymore.

I love my daughter. And I love myself too.

I'm replacing it with a new one, a new badge, a new label of how I'll be.

One that just says:

Leonie.

That's all I ever needed to be.

The Mother I Already Am.

Tell me about the
Mother You Are…
Perfect just as you are!

Dear my Mama,
Thank you for bringing
me into this world.
Thank you for loving
me fiercely, tenderly,
joyously with your
♡ lioness heart.
Thank you for
nurturing my spirit
and encouraging
me to be the
woman I was
meant to be.
Thank you for
being you...

How art healed my mama soul

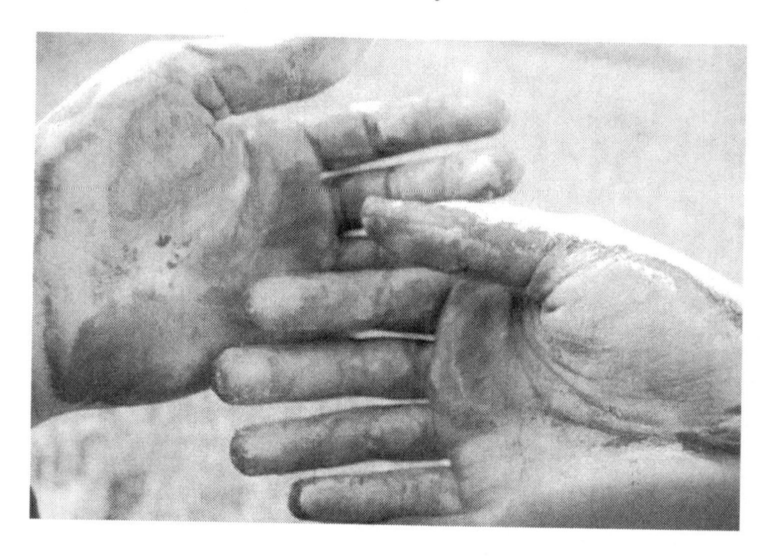

I forgot how healing creating was.

Just how much my soul needs and craves and longs for those moments I have a pen in hand, writing my heart out. Oil pastels smudging my fingertips into rainbows. Colour streaming across the canvas. Paint streaks on my legs.
In these nine months since I became a mama, I forgot.

I forgot to come home.

I forgot that making art wasn't just that fun little hobby of mine that I could put away when I didn't have time.
I forgot that making art was the place I healed.
Making art was the thing that let the stars in me glow.

I forgot creating was breathing. It was to embrace fully my life, my self, my soul.

I forgot.

I put it away in a cupboard.

I closed it with keys to make it baby safe.

And I said to myself, over and over:

I don't have time now.

I was hollow and dream walking.

I wondered where on earth my dreaming juice went. If my sparkle, my lover, had gone on holidays without me, if it had left me for good, if it ever thought of me, if it would ever come back.

I used to be the girl who turned up to parties late, usually with paint on her chin, and go home early because she had a hot date with a canvas that wasn't going to paint itself, you know.

I used to be the girl who had a Things To Do This Life list, and she made them happen, thank you very much.

I used to be the girl who would make stuff wildly and easily. Who had creative projects up every single sleeve. Who had a studio, and a house that became a studio that we lived in.

The afternoon before I gave birth, I was finishing painting a rainbow birthing woman, and was writing & blogging away. And then an owl swooped in, and took my life.

That funny, creative, misshapen life of mine. That one that was so filled with making art and making dreams. A life of my own.

And I became an abalone shell, one that existed to hold this exquisite little being.

A breastfeeding pouch. The bigger spoon.
I became arms and boobs. The night sentinel, and the day sentinel too.

I rushed to the toilet until I gave up on a minute of my own, and took her to the toilet with me. I took tiny showers, and ran out, shampoo in hair, everytime I heard her cry.
Life inverted from My Life That Existed To Serve Me, to The Life That Existed To Serve Another.

It wasn't that I didn't love her.

Oh how I did – and oh, how I do.

How could I not?

She is the brightest star in the sky.

A brave and joyful and sage soul wrapped in the tiniest of growing bodies.

She is a miracle, and is exactly the daughter I knew I would have.

I absolutely, unequivocally needed to have her. Needed to know this path.

Needed to give it all up.

And oh, how I did.

So I sit here, nine months after the Great Earthquake. Hands trembling over the words, staring out the window to yet another summer rainburst.

I gave it up – those things that made me dance – those things that made me me – until I knew I couldn't live a life that wasn't my own.

I did the impossible, and I began carving deep to find and get time – just for me – again.

Time to go home.

And where was home?

It started with a wild and messy imagining, fingerpainted and inked on canvas.

Twenty minutes while babe played at my feet.

And then I grew brave about asking for my sanity, and I started disappearing across the meadow, into town and a little cafe.

Just for two hours.

I write. I doodle without tiny hands reaching up to help my paper disintegrate.

I fill out my own workbook. I start dreaming again. Writing out who I am, what I am grateful for and what I want in aqua, fuscia, lime green, purple.

I have my Folder of Leonie. I keep adding to it. Rainbow tabs.

I do my soul's work.

And I find myself again.

I struggled that I was being selfish.

I struggled that I wasn't a mama who was totally and completely filled just with the purpose of being a mama.
I struggled that that wasn't my idea of The Perfect Mama.

But what I have learned?

This particular constellation of cells – the one they call Leonie – well, she needs and craves her art and creating.

She gets healed by it.

She finds herself again.

She is better for it.

And most of all – she needs herself and her art. The world needs her art too.

So I found the beat of my own step again.
One tripping tune at a time.

One step here, one fumble, one rearrange.
That sparkle inside me? My long lost lover?

I see it sneaking back in.

Little fireflies in my soul.

I'm rewriting my story.

I'm rewriting what it is to be a mama – THIS mama.

I'm telling it again and again.

I nearly lost myself in that great battle, that initiation of becoming a mother.

But I made my way back.

With a pen in hand, writing my heart out. Oil pastels smudging my fingertips into rainbows. Colour streaming across the canvas. Paint streaks on my legs. All pointing the way home.

Making stars in my soul.

Here. Here is where I am.

We women – we need our art. We need to dream.

Something magic happens there, in the space between pen and paper, between paint and canvas... Souls glow, and come alive.

We awaken.

We remember who we are.

We breathe in magic, we breath out joy.

The world becomes glad again.

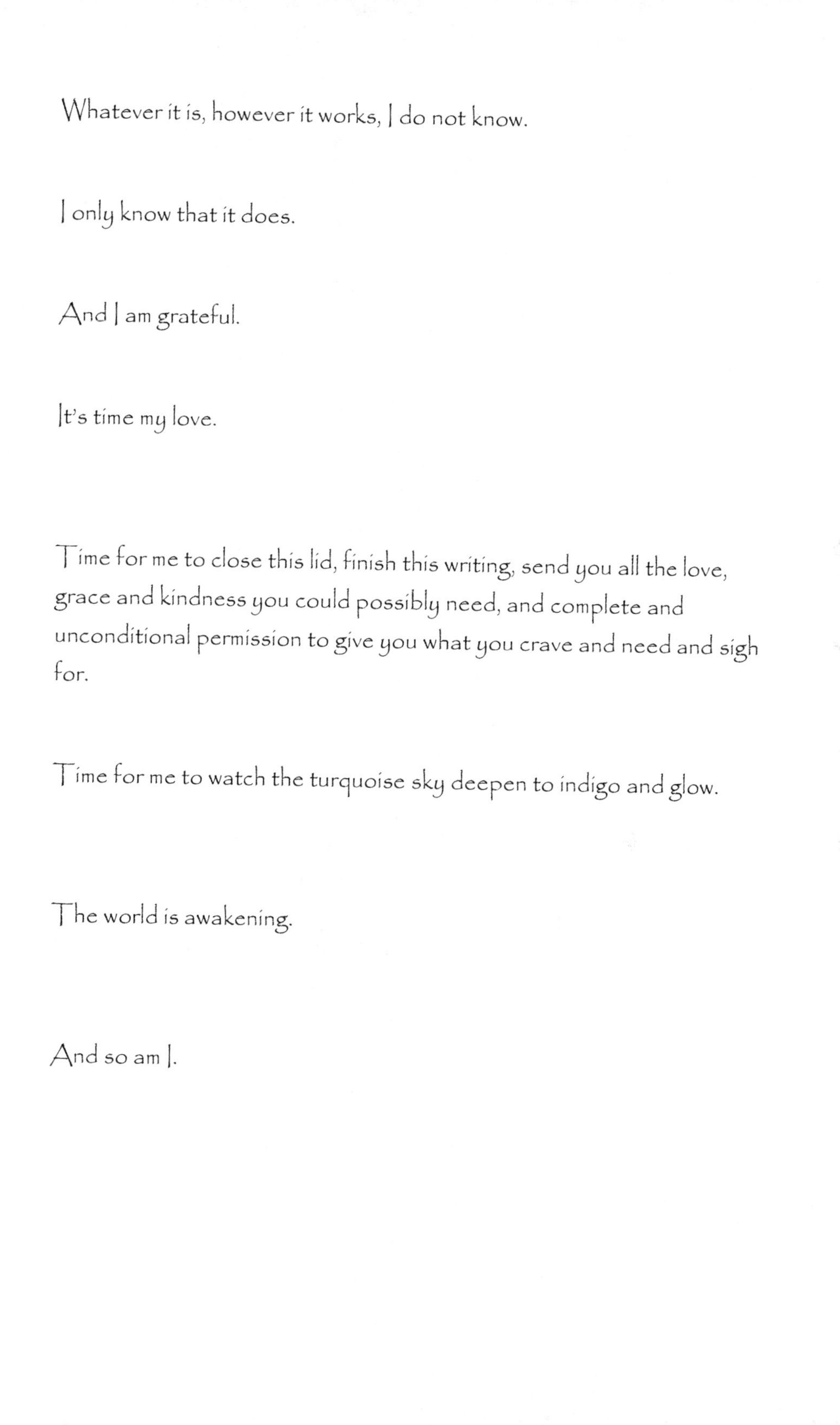

Whatever it is, however it works, I do not know.

I only know that it does.

And I am grateful.

It's time my love.

Time for me to close this lid, finish this writing, send you all the love, grace and kindness you could possibly need, and complete and unconditional permission to give you what you crave and need and sigh for.

Time for me to watch the turquoise sky deepen to indigo and glow.

The world is awakening.

And so am I.

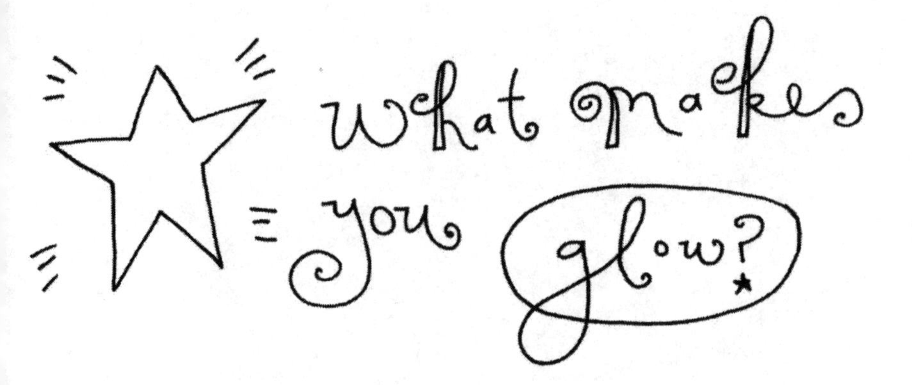
What makes you glow?

Dear You,

You are safe. You are loved. You are held. All will be well. We are supporting you, surrounding, holding you with a thousand angel wings. Act as if you are the most beautiful, precious, loved soul to walk the planet – because you are. If you need our help, please just ask us. We have been by your side since you were born, and before then too. We love you & believe in you…

Love, deeper than the oceans,

Your Angels

The World is Good

Did you know?

Every generation of children gets treated better and better than the last.

I know, I know. I know we beat ourselves up about parenting.

I know we whine about television & how hard everything can be for kids.

And yes, we're still evolving and learning, and we will continue to.

But the thing that makes me sigh a biiiiig exhale of relief?

Knowing that our children are treated better than we were treated. And we were raised more compassionately than our parents were. And our parents were raised more gently than their parents were.

Yes, there are exceptions to the rule. But the HUGE majority is that of love, evolution and healing.

Every generation, we are able to heal even more. Love even more. Take care of our children even more.

Did you know?

That in Australia, women didn't get the right to vote until 1902.

That in 2002, women in Bahrain were given the right to vote.

Look at what has happened in the last 100 years!

My Great Grandmother was not able to vote. I am.

I love that our world is changing & will continue to. And so quickly!!!

Did you know?

Since Kiva.org opened its doors six years ago, over $234 million has been lent from ordinary, everyday people to help people in developing countries grow their businesses.

Did you know the repayment rate of those loans is higher than 99% – higher than the repayment rate for banks in the First World!

We are each changing the world. Helping each other.

Right at the earthy-scented ground level.

Did you know?

That when William Shakespeare was born, he was extraordinary. Not because of the fact that he ended up becoming a famous play write – he was extraordinary simply because he survived. In the century he was born, 25% of children died before the age of 5. But in the year he was born? 66% of children died thanks to the plague.

66%. 2 out of every 3 children.

And now, the plague is pretty much wiped out.

Children are safer and healthier than ever before.

Did you know?

There's a business man in China – Chen Guangbiao. And he's kinda hilarious & flashy & loves publicity.

AND at the same time? His mission is to be the biggest philanthropist in the world.

He wants to be the dude that gives away the most money.

So he drives around & hands out red envelopes filled with cash to people who need them.

And he's trying to get the whole of China to start donating muchos more money.

(And wanna know why? He grew up poor. Some of his siblings starved to death. And so he started working. And he'd earn enough money to pay to go to school. And then earn more so he could pay the tuition for his neighbour's children.)

I want to pash this man something chronic.

Holy guacamole this world is awesome.

Did you know?

Love grows.

Even when people die. Even when relationships end.

Love?

It never leaves us.

It's all around us.

And everytime we foget?

It's like a fish forgetting it is swimming in the sea.

We are swimming in love.

Did you know?

My great aunt was paralysed from polio, and her lover cared for her for all his life.

And that polio – since peaking in the 1940s and 1950s has been eradicated in all but four countries.

Did you know?

That when my eldest brother was growing up with cerebral palsy, there were no support groups here in this small town. No respite. And no special education facilities for teenagers – resulting in him staying until primary school until he was 15.

And that now?

There are services out the wazoo. Families with disabilities are supported and helped and have carers assisting them. My mother is one of them.

So much has changed in one generation.

Did you know?

A couple of months ago, I saw a photo of a child on Facebook. A child that was malnourished.

And so I adopted a child in India. And a buffalo in America. And an Aboriginal Healing Centre in Australia.

And it was the funnest night of "shopping" I ever did.

How much fun is that? We get to help other people! And animals! And missions!!!

All at our fingertips!!!

Motherofgawd, this is pretty much the FUNNEST universe possible!!!!

Did you know?

My Grandmother – the one who has been through 2 World Wars, a Great Depression, losing two husbands, two sons & a grandson – she says that everyday is good?

"Well my darling! I woke up this morning and I was still breathing, so I thought: *Today is a GOOOOOOOOD day!!"*

I saw her up the street just before. She's 94 & was shopping & flirting. I offered to drive her back to her house, but she wanted to walk.

She was dressed in white moccasins, a dazzling white tailored skirt, pearls, a soft pink mohair jumper & was accessorised with gigantic pink-framed hipster sunglasses & iridescent dangly shell earrings.

"Granny, you look GORGEOUS! You have the best style in the WORLD!"

"Well my darling! I take after my grand daughter!"

P.S. My Grandmother is not just my grandmother – she's yours too. She holds the whole world in her strong, bangle-adorned arms & sings

"Youuuuuu are sooooooooo beautiful....

to meeeeee........"

Did you know?

That you don't have to worry about the world.

And if there's something that you'd like to change, you can change it.

You can turn all that excess energy – of fear, of worry, of pain – and channel it into something that transforms. And heals. And blooms.

And it can be ding dang FUN.

Did you know?

I am in love with the world.

It's pretty much the best thing ever.

So much hope. SO much possibility. So much transformation and love and kindness.

And it just gets better and better.

I am a Goddess.

← draw yourself in here!

You are a Goddess

Inside you is a wise, powerful, beautiful Goddess ★ You are a modern day Athena, Kali, Persephone & aphrodite ☆ Inside you is all the wisdom you need ★ You are here for a deeply important reason ★ your journey is sacred ★ you touch this world with your gifts & presence

☆★ You are a goddess ★☆

Want to dive
Deeper
into
being
a Goddess?

Free Stuff!

- ★ Free TV shows online
- ★ Free Podcast
- ★ Thousands of free articles on Creativity, Spirituality, Business , Happiness & Mamahood
- ★ Free weekly e-zine filled with tips on making your life + business shine!
- ★ Free mini video workshops
- ★ Free meditations
- ★ Free ebooks & posters

Visit

www.LeonieDawson.com

The Amazing Life & Biz Shop!

E-Courses

Business Goddess E-Course

A complete guide–over 190 pages!!– on how to build a beautiful booming business for your creative & spiritual passions. You'll learn ways to make money, the blueprint of how I took my goddess hobby to a 6-figure business within 3 years & 100+ ways to market your business!

"What I love about the Business Goddess course is that it's fun, lush and soups-to-nuts on what you need to have a love-filled, fit-you and successful business. Highly recommended!"

- Jennifer Louden, Oprah show expert + best-selling author

Order now at www.AmazingBizandLifeAcademy.com

How To Hire, Grow + Keep A Shining Six Figure Team

At a certain point, you'll become the bottleneck in your business – you're not able to grow your business because you are out of time, energy + sanity. It's so, so deeply important that you find the right people to support you on your team. I'm going to share with you the exact details about when to hire, who to hire, how to hire without making mistakes, how to develop + grow your team so they become truly exceptional, + how to keep them forever. And you know I'm an open book, so I'll share with you the intimate details that many other business owners won't – all for the purpose of helping you grow your own beautiful business as quickly + joyfully as possible. This guide will help you create an amazing team, supercharge your business growth + bring you so much more joy, love + support into your life.

Order now at www.AmazingBizandLifeAcademy.com

Radiant Goddess E-Course

A 21-day nutrition, movement & meditation journey to revitalise your body, mind & soul! You'll be guided by gorgeous menu plans, movement plans, spirit + inspiration projects, and meditations to guide you as you reawaken your Radiant Goddess self. This is perfect if you're ready to be moving, meditating, eating & discovering in a *joyful, spirited goddess way*. Ready to feel blissed out, inspired & radiant?

Creative Goddess E-Course

A six-week guided journey to discover the Creative Goddess in you! This e-course is both practical + spiritual, and will help you discover (or remember!) that you were born an artist, art can help you heal, creativity can make your spirituality bloom in new & beautiful ways, and that *you really are a creative goddess*. If you're ready to remember how inspired, wise & courageous you are, this journey is for you!

Order now at www.AmazingBizandLifeAcademy.com

Create Your Goddess Haven program

A six-week adventure for when you're wanting & needing & *craving* a space that is a true haven for the Goddess in you! You'll use space clearing techniques to make your space's energy sparkle. You'll banish your feelings of overwhelm & "where do I start?" powerlessness. You'll be empowered with all of the wisdom, tools & techniques you need to make your space feel & look amazing *to you.*

Order now at www.AmazingBizandLifeAcademy.com

Meditations

Divine Dreaming Meditation Kit

A meditation kit to help you get to sleep easier & have more divine dreams.

This meditation will help you drift into slumber more easily, have wise + healing dreams, feel more revitalised when you awaken & have *way more glorious days* because your nights are so much more nourishing!

"In short, buying your meditation was the best money I'd spent in some time."
- Rebekah

"Your meditation was the best I have ever experienced. I wish I could wake up to your meditations every morning."
- Melanie

Order now at www.AmazingBizandLifeAcademy.com

Releasing Fears Meditation Kit

Use this meditation to let go, be free, and *shine*. This meditation is powerful for whenever you're feeling stuck, lost or down from any old pains and fears you may have. You'll fell less stuck by your fears, stronger and clearer, and so much freer to chase your big, beautiful dreams!

Chakra Healing Goddess Meditation Kit

A complete meditation to cleanse your chakras, heal & feel gorgeously light & shiny! This is a powerful tool for whenever you need healing. It will help you activate physical, spiritual & emotional healing all over your body. You'll have more clarity, feel more joyful, and feel more connected with your angels + the Goddess inside you!

Order yours now at www.AmazingBizandLifeAcademy.com

Holy Dinger Uber Deep Zennifying Meditation Kit

Go deep into zen goddess mode & get brilliant moments of insight. After trying a bazillion meditation techniques, I found a technique that *really worked* for me. And as soon as I learned it, I wanted to share it with you. Just a moment of meditation is worth a hundred moments without – and whether you've got 5, 10 or 20 minutes (or more), this meditation technique can help you get totally zennified!

Kits + Workbooks

Create Your Amazing Year Workbook: Life + Business Editions!

A complete workbook, calendar & planner to dream, plan & grow your gorgeous year in life and business!

Featured in the Huffington Post, these yearly workbooks are a perennial best seller.

This is the perfect place to begin or continue your journey. Priced at just $9.95 each, these workbooks are incredibly powerful and an essential workbook for every woman.

They've helped thousands of women transform their lives and businesses every single year and create their own dreams come true.

Get yours NOW at www.AmazingWorkbook.com **now!**

Sacred Space Clearing

Seven ways to clear negative energy & help your home lift you up! Whether your goal is to feel happier in your space, get more money (or creativity or love) flowing through your space, or just feel calmer and more at ease in your space, the sacred space clearing techniques in this kit can get you there.

Creating With Kids

We mamas, we need our art. And we need to include our kids in it too. And it's different from ABF (Art Before Kids). It takes a whole new level of art skills, tools, perspectives & set-up. So Ostara & I decided to invite you around… to paint with us, to spill water & eat paint & laugh wildly & get rained on… and find out what it is to be CREATIVE MAMA GODDESSES.

AMAZING BIZ + LIFE ACADEMY

What would it be like to get all of these e-courses, meditations & workbooks? Easily & super affordably?

To have at your fingertips all you need to be a radiant, creative, wise, joyful Goddess?

Then what would it be like to have your very own Sacred Circle and mastermind to help you grow your very own amazing life and business? Available to you whenever and wherever you need it – right at your computer?

Join the Amazing Biz and Life Academy for the miracles to begin in YOUR life + biz!

Get ***ALL*** of Leonie's programs – incredibly powerful e-courses, meditations & workbooks. PLUS a year-round women's circle and mastermind!

You get **thousands of dollars of powerful programs to change your life + biz at a fraction of the cost!**

Join 4000+ women now and

become an Academy member:

www.AmazingBizandLifeAcademy.com

About the Author

Leonie Dawson is a mentor to women wanting to create + grow massively successful and heart-centered creative + soulful businesses. She is also an author, retreat leader, visual artist, mama and guide for the tens of thousands who receive her free "AMAZING BIZ + AMAZING LIFE" eZine each week.

Leonie has taught alongside such luminaries as Arielle Ford, Julia Cameron, Gay Hendricks and SARK. Leonie has coached tens of thousands of women to create their own incredible lives and businesses including crystal healers, celebrities, coaches, best-selling authors, award-winning singers, fitness experts, yoga teachers, multiple-six-figure entrepreneurs and artists.

Previously, Leonie has worked as editor of the Australian Government's business website business.gov.au which garnered a United Nations award during her time there. She has also previously worked in Minister's Offices at Parliament House and as a legal secretary. Leonie was formerly a top-achieving economics + art history student at Australian National University before dropping out to become a successful artist.

Purposeful, passionate & unendingly prolific, published her first book at 22 and has gone on to create a solo art exhibition, lead women's circles and retreats, create popular e-courses, workbooks + meditations. and create the Amazing Biz & Life Academy.

In the process, she has built a half-million dollar a year company that doubles in size each year and helps thousands of women every single year. Her mission is to help as many earth angels – women with creative or spiritual gifts – to have profoundly profitable businesses so they may nourish themselves and heal the world.

Leonie has walked labyrinths in the moonlight, wept atop mountains in the middle of a storm, danced with a baby in an old cow shed as a Filipino tribal chief sang, and once married herself in a public commitment ceremony — witnessed by goddess maidens of honor that she'd met on the Internet.

YOU ARE A
goddess